Liz Jazwiec's First Award-Winning Book: A Treat You Don't Want to Miss!

Yes, you *can* create a positive workforce in negative times, says strategist and author Liz Jazwiec, RN. But first you have to get real about how tough a job in healthcare really is—and about the negative things you and staff members do to make it even tougher.

In the award-winning *Eat That Cookie!: Make Workplace Positivity Pay Off...for Individuals, Teams and Organizations*, Liz does just that. In her darkly humorous, ever-so-slightly sarcastic style, the former ER nurse builds a case for the powerful benefits of a positive workplace.

Readers will learn:
- Why hokeyness—i.e., smiley face cookies and no-negativity days—actually works
- How to decree and enforce "mandatory fun" so that it's really, well, *fun*
- How not to succumb to "process paralysis"
- Why victim-thinking is so destructive and how to eliminate it from the organization
- How to stop judging shoe-heel smashers, pants unzippers, and other irritating patients

Put the tips in *Eat That Cookie!* into practice and you'll be amazed by the rapid improvements you see—in terms of energy, focus, productivity, and yes, happiness.

Hey Cupcake! We Are ALL Leaders

Liz Jazwiec has done it again! Her second book, *Hey Cupcake! We Are ALL Leaders*, is as funny and inspiring as her first. In it, she explains that we'll *all* eventually be called on to lead someone—whether it's a department, a shift, a project team, or a new employee—and delves into the traits and skills needed to do it effectively. In her trademark slightly sarcastic (and often hilarious) voice, she provides learned-the-hard-way insights that will benefit leaders in every industry and at every level.

Readers will learn:
- How to GET OVER IT and help your employees get over it, too (Liz coins a new phrase, "Pink Robe Rage")
- Liz's amusing approach to managing change (it involves the acronym BARF)
- How to deal with problem employees and button pushers (Evil Queens, Wicked Poisoners, Calamity Janes, and more)
- A quick and easy "test" that will help you hire the right people
- How an ugly red nightgown can teach us to *tell* others what we really need

To order copies at a special bulk discount rate, please visit www.firestarterpublishing.com or call 866-354-3473.

Listen to *Eat That Cookie!* and *Hey Cupcake!* Straight from the Author

Both *Eat That Cookie!* and *Hey Cupcake!* are available in audio-book format and are narrated by Liz Jazwiec herself. Available through Amazon, Audible, and iTunes.

SERVICE EXCELLENCE IS AS EASY AS PIE

(Perception Is Everything)

Liz Jazwiec

Award-Winning Author of *Eat That Cookie!*
and *Hey Cupcake! We Are ALL Leaders*

Published by:
Fire Starter Publishing
913 Gulf Breeze Parkway, Suite 6
Gulf Breeze, FL 32561
Phone: 850-934-1099
Fax: 850-934-1384
www.firestarterpublishing.com

ISBN: 978-1-622-18001-1

Library of Congress Control Number: 2014941187

Printed in the United States of America

I dedicate this book to:

Frank Jazwiec

The Joy of my day
The Light of my night
The Love of my life

Table of Contents

Foreword

Sometimes it seems everything I read lately about healthcare is "doom and gloom." And it's true that we are undergoing some big shifts. Yet, instead of looking at this as a negative, I feel challenged by the opportunity. Heck, we save lives, we care for patients in the times of their greatest need, we research new treatments that give people hope. We can, and will, adjust to the "new normal."

Yes, the challenges we face are huge. Healthcare organizations have moved from operating in a state of episodic change to one of continuous change—and as John Kotter has famously noted, that requires a whole different set of skills and a much higher level of urgency.

This doesn't apply only to healthcare. The global economy and social media have changed the way customers in all industries do business and the way they view the services they receive. Meanwhile, serious economic pressures force companies to get more done with fewer and fewer resources. These changes demand relentless high performance.

All of this means today's employees are feeling pretty overwhelmed. And the stress we're under can put us into an "all business" frame of mind—meaning we're so focused on the quality of our products and services that it can be tough to *also* think about the customer's perception. But not only do we need to think about it, we need to integrate this focus on perception into our culture.

In healthcare, the way patients perceive their care is especially critical because of its direct link to the bottom line.

For example, an organization's results on HCAHPS and CGCAHPS surveys—which measure the patient experience—now affect its reimbursement. And, of course, the increased transparency will impact where patients choose to go and which physicians they choose to see.

Now for the good news. Improving perception (and making sure it stays improved) doesn't take a lot of extra work or even extra time. In fact, as Liz Jazwiec points out, it's often the little things that make the biggest impact on how patients and customers view their experience.

In healthcare, this might mean narrating a procedure in a way that relieves a patient's anxiety, or "managing up" the next person she will see, or (as Liz describes in Chapter 10) providing soft blankets for family members waiting in the visitors' lounge. In retail, it might mean remembering a customer's name and style preferences. In hospitality, it might mean sending an inexpensive bottle of wine to a customer's room in honor of her birthday.

At Studer Group we find that organizations may provide the same great quality and service they always have, yet when they start communicating and setting expectations in a different way, the way patients perceive their care changes. A few key words can completely change their experience. That's service excellence.

Doing these things for patients and customers feels good to employees, too. In fact, it's incredibly energizing and rewarding. Making *them* happier makes *you* happier. You start looking for ways to provide even better service. You start connecting (or reconnecting) to why you wanted to do this work in the first place. Your work starts to feel a lot more meaningful.

What I'm describing here is exactly what leaders mean when they talk about engagement. Without engaged employees there is no way to do all we need to do to keep up with the demands of our disruptive external environment. To provide care that feels like care, you have to actually *care.* You can't fake it.

That's why Liz is the perfect person to bring the subject of service excellence to life. She never fakes *anything.* She writes the way she comes across in real life—with brutal honesty and a slightly dark sense of humor—and that's why her message hits home. You'll see yourself in her words and examples, and you'll see how you might do an even better job of serving those you're called to serve.

I hope you'll find this book as inspiring as I do. I hope you'll read it and—like I did—feel grateful for the opportunity to make a difference in the lives of others.

Quint Studer

Introduction

So, here is my book about service excellence. It's funny that it is my third book, because service is where it all began. When I first started my speaking career, all of my talks were centered on patient satisfaction. You see, everything I learned about culture (which I wrote about in *Eat That Cookie!*) and leadership (which I wrote about in *Hey Cupcake! We Are ALL Leaders*) was discovered while leading a very resistant Emergency Department team in improving patient satisfaction.

From Rebellious Resistance to Revelation

For those of you who haven't read my other books or heard me speak, let me tell you that when I say I led a resistant team, I mean that I was the ring leader. I was *by far* the most resistant. I despised the thought of customer service and patient satisfaction; I was convinced that those things had no place in healthcare. I was an ED nurse and firmly felt that our only job was to "save lives and stamp out disease." I never worried about patients' or families' impressions or perceptions. I didn't care about their "experience." I truly believed that outcomes and results were all that mattered. Get the picture?

And then one day while I was merrily working as the Emergency Department director at Holy Cross Hospital in Chicago (okay, maybe not just one day, and probably not all that merrily...), things changed. There was a new executive team at the hospital. Mark Clement was the new chief executive officer, and he brought in a man by the name of Quint Studer to be our senior vice president. And somehow, without consulting with me, they embarked on a huge patient satisfaction initiative.

I was far from being on board; actually, I was extremely resistant. I thought Mark and Quint had taken leave of their senses. I distinctly remember being at a meeting where one of them actually said that there was no reason why customer service in our hospital could not be as good as the service at Disney World.

WHAT?!? Holy Cross is a hospital on the South Side of Chicago. Songs (and not the happy kind) have been written about the South Side of Chicago. It's tough, I mean, *really* tough. "Disney World, HA!" I wanted to say. "Hey, you want to see Disney World? I'll show you Disney World. Why don't you come to our Emergency Department on a Friday night, say around midnight? You'll see Disney World, Adventureland,

Never-Never Land, oh and hey…would you like to have your picture taken with Goofy?!? Check out Bed 5."

Yep, it was that rebellious resistance to service that got me very close to being fired…twice! People always ask, "Liz, how did you come to truly embrace patient satisfaction as the 'right' way? Did you have an epiphany? Some type of mystical revelation?"

"Um, no," I always reply. "I was just about fired…TWICE!"

In fact, the second time I was almost fired (I was given 90 days to improve service or GET OUT), Quint moved the hospital superstar, Don Dean, into my office. At the time, Don was the director of Ambulatory Services, and it didn't take a vivid imagination to figure out why he was repositioned in the Emergency Services offices. Yep, Quint's plan was that when my 90 days were up, good ol' Don would be right there and ready to take over. (P.S., almost 20 years later, Don and I are still good friends, although that first year was pretty rough for Don!)

I was literally shoved into service and so was my team. (There is more about this story in my first book, *Eat That Cookie!*) We did not go willingly, but as we did a better job of creating improved patient experiences, I discovered that the team's morale improved. It was amazing to witness. And I did finally have a revelation. We all go into "service" professions because we want to make a difference in people's lives.

Certainly this is true for healthcare, but it also applies to education, social service, civil service, and so many more professions. Making a difference, making people less anxious, making

people feel better, making people feel noticed and special…
that's what improves a team's morale. Those are also the components of any good service initiative.

It can't be that simple, you think. But guess what? IT IS. That is the reason why I first started lecturing about service. I felt as though I had uncovered a great secret. After being so annoyed with "customer service" and so resistant to "patient satisfaction," I realized that *it wasn't that hard*. I wanted to shout it from the rooftops to all my sisters and brothers, first in nursing, and then to the masses: "Guess what? This service stuff is not hard. It's really easy! You can get administration off of your back once and for all! I know the answer to the riddle."

Like most riddles, the answer is so easy once you figure it out. *Improving patient satisfaction or customer service is not about improving outcomes or results; it is about changing people's perceptions and creating better impressions.* (I will discuss this concept in depth in the first three chapters of this book.)

The Real Enemy Isn't "Difficult" –It's "Different."

When I first started speaking about implementing service strategies and creating a service culture, people in the audience were irritated at me. They said, "You are making this sound far too simple." I even heard some of those infamous "This insults me professionally"'s.

I was shocked. I thought I was bringing everyone good news. But then it dawned on me: All my talk about "we don't have to change outcomes; we simply have to change perceptions" was not only too basic—it was also wildly different from anything that was currently being done.

And for most of us, "different" is a much bigger obstacle than "difficult." Heck, in healthcare we *love* difficult. Think about it: We take the simplest things and make them difficult. Ever been to a committee meeting on policy revision?!? Yeah, we LOVE difficult.

But different, well, now you are going to find BIG resistance. I remember when we first told our team at Holy Cross to start saying "hi" in the hallways. Whoa—big resistance. I can recall a meeting where a couple of people on my team were upset. "Why should we have to say 'hi' in the hallways?" they demanded.

"I don't know," I answered, "but it seems to make a difference and IT'S NOT THAT HARD! So just do it!" I mean seriously, could you think of anything easier than saying hi? And yet, it was initially met with huge resistance.

It is that sort of resistance that has made service initiatives fail. It is that sort of opposition to doing things differently that keeps teams from achieving their goals.

Making Service Stick

Sometimes organizations will ask me if I can come in and "motivate" their teams with a presentation. I always answer the same: "No, I believe motivation is more than a 60-minute talk; however, I do believe I can lower your team's resistance to your service initiatives. Once the resistance is gone, the service piece is easy."

And that is why this is my third book. I have always wanted to write a book about improving service excellence, but I felt that until I covered the areas of culture (*Eat That Cookie!*) and leadership (*Hey Cupcake! We Are ALL Leaders*), the service stuff wouldn't stick. However, once you create a positive culture and develop leaders who can take the team to the next level, the service stuff isn't really all that tough to implement.

So here I am, back to wanting to shout it from the rooftops. Achieving service excellence is not an unattainable, lofty, unrealistic goal. It is really so very simple: Improve your patients' and customers' perceptions, and shazam! Your task is easily accomplished.

Some of the chapters in this book will surprise you, especially when I talk about forgetting outcomes and working on perception. Some will just be a really good refresher with a "Liz" twist. Hopefully *all* of them will give you simple, practical ideas to improve perceptions and impressions, and to make service excellence easy for you and your team.

Insert Your Experience Here!

Please, please, PLEASE, as you read this book, don't get hung up on patient satisfaction versus customer service versus student engagement versus client relations. Yes, I know that not all fields are the same and that there are differences in the people we serve. When I talk about improving service excellence, I *always* mean all of the above. So whether I use an example about a student, a patron in a restaurant, a hospital visitor, or something else, I hope you'll relate the story to the work you do. If you think about how to apply each of my anecdotes to your particular field, you'll have the tools you need to make service excellence less difficult and more attainable for you and your team.

Understanding Perception: The "Quality Vs. Service" Controversy

First, a question for you: If your mother were sick, and you had the choice between a nurse who could interpret the heart monitor, start an IV with one try, and do the appropriate treatments or some SMILING IDIOT, which one would you go with? I don't know about YOU, but I would take the nurse who knew what she was doing every time!

I would choose the nurse like me—and I am definitely no smiling idiot! One time this guy complained to me, "I have been here for over eight hours trying to figure out why I have this headache, and after all the x-rays, a CT scan, and the brain doctor exam, you tell me nothing is wrong. What the heck?" I was so tempted to say, "Oh, no, sorry, you have a brain tumor. Ha! Now does that make you feel better?"

Then of course there's the all-time favorite (resurrected from the past): "I'm here to save your ass...not kiss it."

Yes, the above comment is something that I have said (okay, really, *really* WANTED to say) back in the days when I didn't understand that quality and service—aka, outcome and perception—were different.

And when the distinction between service and quality is not clear, creating excellent customer/patient experiences seems impossible. Even well-meaning organizations with dedicated teams still do not achieve service excellence.

After speaking with countless organizations about all the initiatives and strategies they have used to try to improve customer service and enhance patient experience, I am still surprised that so many continue to struggle. Why is that, exactly? Well, while there are a handful of universal issues that all organizations wrestle with, the one that is evident everywhere is the tendency to lump quality and service together.

Organizations think of these two concepts as the same thing and even combine them (as in "Service Quality"). Yet—get ready for a newsflash—they're *not*.

Wait...What!? I can hear some of you saying. *This statement flies in the face of what we have believed for years. Everyone knows there is a link between quality and service.*

Okay, hold on. I am not disagreeing that service and quality aren't, in fact, linked. (They are.) My objective here is simply to describe how they work together, while standing alone as two separate concepts. Overall, I believe that the customer experience is made up of a combination of both quality (outcomes and results) as well as service (impressions and perceptions).

Two Sides of the Same Coin

Service and quality are two sides of the same coin, if you will, but just like all coins, each side is different. Really, they are. Take a quarter out of your pocket. See, one side is a big head, and if you have a "new" quarter, the other side has a picture of a building or monument, or the outline of a state. Same coin, different pictures. With me so far?

Now, let's look at your quarter in even more detail. The amount is stamped on only one side, so some might say that it is the more "valuable" side. However, if you have one of the "new" 50 state quarters, the other side—the one with the building or state—might be more collectible. So which side of the quarter is *actually* more important? The side with the dollar amount (let's say it represents quality because it's tied to results) or the side with the state-specific picture (it represents service because the picture represents something about that state that makes a positive impression on its residents and visitors)?

This is a silly example, of course, because neither side is more important. People who argue for one over the other would be fools, because it is one coin. It can't be separated! The side you prefer doesn't matter.

In my humble opinion (okay, maybe more brash than humble), we have all spent a lot of time getting an understanding of the quality side of the coin. I think we do a great job of focusing on our outcomes and results. However, most of us have not devoted as much time to understanding the service side of the coin: the impressions and, most importantly, the perceptions we create. It's time to correct that imbalance.

Maybe you're resistant to think of quality and service as equally important. *If we put service and quality on the same continuum,* you say, *quality always will trump service, because quality is an indicator of actual outcomes, not people's opinions.* Okay, I'll grant you that service won't "win" against quality. But I will also say that if you insist on separating the two and pitting them against each other, you're approaching service excellence all wrong.

If you really want to improve, you need to think of quality and service as separate but equal. A focus on one improves your chance of being successful with the other, and vice versa.

Quality Is a Given. (Duh!)

Now that we've established that quality and service are both important, I want to help you understand the differences between the two concepts. Here's the angle that really helped me: Think about quality as reflecting the mental and physical aspects of patient care. For example, the patient understood their discharge instructions, the patient's wound healed, blah,

blah, blah. Quality is all about metrics that are measured across the country: medication, fall rates, nosocomial infections, etc. These things add up to outcomes and results.

Now, think about service as affecting the spiritual and the emotional side of things. For instance, I was treated with respect, everyone was nice, etc….all the things that form the patient's perceptions and impressions of their care. Like most of us who have been trained as scientists, you may think that this spiritual, emotional stuff is "hex whammy, goofy, mystical rubbish."

But there's a lot more to "spiritual, emotional stuff" than that. That's because quality is a given. People assume it is there. They expect great outcomes and improved results from all types of organizations, so we don't get any credit for achieving those things.

Believe it or not, I've had a nurse say, "Liz, can you please tell me why someone isn't happy to come in to the hospital with a serious illness, be treated by a team of professionals who know what they're doing, get things done, go home, and have a better outcome? Why doesn't that make them happy?" Because that's what they expect!

Now, we all know that when you are on the "inside" of any industry, things look a little different. You know that quality is *not* a given. For instance, if you work in healthcare and have to have your blood drawn tomorrow, do you know which phlebotomist you'd ask? Of course. And if you are an educator, you know what teacher you are hoping your son has for first grade.

Of course you have preferences about these things. As I said, we're on the inside, and we know the truth. But that's not true for most people. Their assumption is that no matter who cooks their food, no matter who does their ultrasound, no matter who teaches the class, no matter who performs *whatever*, the outcome is going to be the right one. (And it *should* be.)

Basically, it's nearly impossible to overdeliver on quality because—as I've pointed out—people expect perfection. What do you think would happen if a hospital launched a marketing campaign tomorrow centered on a message like, *Come to our hospital—almost everybody gets the right medicine!* Or, *Come to our facility—there's a very slim chance your grandma will fall and break her hip in our hallway!* Or, *Most people don't leave here with more infections than they came in with!* Think those slogans would work? HA!

An Unfair Double Whammy

Think about this: Practically every quality problem is accompanied by a related service issue. So you get zero credit when the outcome and results are perfect and a double negative when they're not. This feels really unfair, doesn't it?

For example, let's say that Grandma falls and breaks her hip in your hallway. You not only have a quality issue (broken hip=bad outcome), now you have a service issue (the family's impression that the staff doesn't care and the hospital is terrible=bad perception).

Here's my point: Instead of being judged by our outcomes and results, people judge us based on their perceptions and impressions. And as unfair as this scenario may seem, most of us are the exact same way when we step outside of our industry.

It's All About the Cup Holder...

People say, "But, Liz, healthcare is life or death...people ought to be happy for the quality they receive, not take it for granted." But when we're outside of healthcare, we assume that quality is a given, too. Here, I'm going to share an example that I think will help you understand where our patients are coming from.

Let's look at the auto industry. I'm thinking that when a car is built, there are some quality aspects of its construction that are of life-and-death importance. Don't you agree? Step on the brakes, and the car stops. Drive down the street, and the tires don't fly off. Put the key in the ignition, and the car doesn't blow up. Those are some significant quality issues, and I, for one, am hoping somebody is checking them off.

However, when I buy a new car, those are not the things I'm excited about, are they? I don't go to my friends and say, "Look at my new car! I step on this pedal and it stops!" Instead, I look for other things. And I'm not alone.

For example, I know a man who told me, "My wife wouldn't let me buy an SUV because of the cup holder. I was ready to sign on the dotted line, but then she test drove the car and said, 'I can't reach the cup holder.' The salesman goes, 'Ma'am, it has a superior engine; the quality of it is just remarkable.' But my wife said, 'I don't care. I'm not going to get in that car every single morning and not be able to reach my coffee. The cup holder is not right.' That poor sales guy was ready to shoot either her or himself!"

The auto industry has "insider information," too. Have you ever heard, "Don't buy a car built on a Monday or a Friday"? If so, you probably received that advice from people on the inside…right? It's because they know. But still, how many of us "outsiders" have actually used the day of the week as a criterion when buying a car?

Personally, I choose my cars based on the things that are important to me. What color is it? How big is the trunk? And the most important thing of all: How *cool* do I look driving this thing? Now, I'm willing to bet every last penny I have that people on the inside of the auto industry are saying, "Lady, you have your priorities screwed up!" Right?

Sound familiar? This is exactly what we want to say to our patients sometimes! But remember—we focus on trivial things like cup holders when we buy a car because we *expect* certain quality standards to be present, no matter what. If those quality standards *aren't* there, we are going to have a serious service problem, aren't we?

For instance, let's say I get in my car one day, put the key in the ignition, turn it on, and BLAM! It blows up! I hope we not only have a HUGE quality problem, but also one heck of a service problem. I hope the next time my family goes to buy a car they say, "Didn't Liz blow up in a Buick? Hmm, maybe we should look at a Chrysler or Toyota…something different this time."

I'll say it one more time: The people we serve are the same. Quality is an expectation, so people judge us based on their impressions and perceptions. Their opinions are based on their emotions—which are often influenced by how convenient the metaphorical cup holders are!

…and Not Falling off Space Mountain.

Okay, one more analogy. What's Disney World's number-one priority?
- Making people happy? No. Sorry, Mickey.
- Making people feel like valued guests? No again.
- Selling as much stuff as possible? You might think… but still no.

Disney World's number-one priority is safety. Of course it is. Think about it: You're on Space Mountain and you fall off, breaking your leg in the process. No matter how many people are dressed up like cute little animals saying, "Hi! Have a nice day!" …you're not having one!

I'm not saying the work that any of you do is like the work that happens at Disney World. But the people who walk through our doors are very much the same people who walk through the turnstiles of the Magic Kingdom. Aren't they? Yes, they are.

The public who assumes they won't be flung off a ride is the same one who assumes we are going to keep them safe, that we're going to do the right thing for them at the right time. Yep—they're the same public who evaluates their experience with us using criteria that we "insiders" might see as trivial or unfair.

So here's the good news: It is not all that hard to improve perception. I am going to spend the rest of this book sharing simple things we can all do to improve perception, make great impressions, and create outstanding service excellence.

But first, at the risk of beating a dead (and maybe even buried) horse, you have to understand that you can't fix service by improving outcomes or results. If you're still not convinced, turn the page and read the next chapter!

2

Improving Perception: Stories from the Front Lines

There are so many misconceptions in our industry about quality and service and our role in improving both. Believe me, I see (and hear) evidence of this every day.

You can't fix service by improving quality! Yes, I said it again. I have to, because even though I have been telling people this for over 20 years, a tremendous amount still believe that not only is it possible to fix service by improving quality; it's the only way!

Just a few months ago, I was having lunch with a group of physicians who were talking about patient satisfaction and HCAHPS. One physician started our conversation by pointing at me and saying, "It isn't fair for anyone in healthcare to be held accountable for service measures, because they are out of our control."

"Do tell," I responded as I picked at my 1,000th chicken Caesar salad.

"I have proof," the physician gloated.

"Really?" *Hmm, now this ought to be good (or at least better than this sad salad)*, I thought. I put my fork down.

"Yes," he went on. "I just read a study showing that over 80 percent of patients who have had a knee replacement can't accurately recall their weight-bearing instructions as little as one week after discharge. The study was conducted by home health physical therapists who, on their first home visits, asked their patients about weight bearing. Of course, the therapists knew what the physicians' orders were from the record. And in this study, over 80 percent of the patients were *wrong* when telling the therapist not only what they were told upon discharge, but what they had been doing at home!" By the end of this speech, the physician looked positively triumphant.

"Interesting," I replied. "Please go on."

The physician looked surprised. "THAT'S it!"

"What?" Clearly I was missing something.

"That's it," he insisted. "That's why we can't be responsible for patient satisfaction, because in just this one example, we gave the patients good information, but most of them didn't follow it at home. So they probably had more pain or less mobility than they should have had, and that most *definitely* made them unhappy. How can a physician be responsible for that?!?"

I did my very best head nod and thought to myself, *Okay, be quiet. There is not enough time romaining* (ha, I know, a bad salad pun!) *in this session for me to explain things to this misguided man.*

Believing that I agreed with him, my lunch companion sat back in his chair, somewhat puffed up and proud. I thought to myself, *Wow, this guy really doesn't get the difference between quality and service.*

Science Isn't Always the Answer.

The physician I described in the previous story certainly isn't alone in his confusion. I encountered another hospital leader who said, "We can prove that our patients are crazy!"

"Really?" I asked. Again, I knew I just *had* to hear this story, especially since this wasn't a psych hospital.

The leader told me, "We decreased our turnaround time by 25 percent and saw no improvement…absolutely *no* improvement…in patient satisfaction scores."

I said, "That's because you did a *quality* improvement. A turnaround time is an outcome. It's a result. You did nothing to manage the patient's expectations. You did nothing to change the customer's perception."

As expected, I got a blank stare in return.

So because perceptions and outcomes are different, we have to use different approaches in order to improve each one. When we work on improving quality, we have to employ a scientific process because we are affecting outcomes and results and, most importantly, patients' lives.

So, you can't just say, "Go try that," or, "Oh, the guy died…I guess it doesn't work." When it comes to quality, there has to be a scientific method to our madness. Believe me, I am not against gathering and acting on evidence. It's the backbone of our industry and is responsible for saving countless lives. I love evidence!

All I'm saying is that when we work on improving service, we *don't* have to use a scientific process. That's because we're not affecting patients' lives; we're affecting their *perception*. We're trying to change their impressions, their feelings, and their emotions. What we need to do is think about how best to highlight our quality tactics to our patients. When we do this well, we'll positively impact their perception.

I've noticed that in many organizations, especially academic ones, "the more scientific we are" tends to correlate with "the more we want to fix service by improving quality." Yes, I'm all for performance improvement, but (I'll say it again!) don't expect to see a resulting improvement in patient satisfaction.

So, if you don't fix service with process, how *do* you fix it? With action! You can take quick, immediate action and forget the long, drawn-out scientific process, because no one is going to get hurt. If you're like the team in my next story, though, you might have to work on loosening up a bit first.

Just Smell the Flowers, Dang It!

I was speaking with a hospital first impression team. First impression teams usually consist of folks in valet parking and security, at the information desks and switchboards, and in admissions and ER registrations, etc. As I was working with this particular team, I said to them, "You know, you might want to order a fresh flower arrangement once a week for your information desk, just to kind of perk things up, have a nice impact."

Do you know that someone on that team raised their hand and said, "Liz, do you have any scientific data to back that up?"

If you are chuckling now, it's because you have been on those kinds of teams. You know, the ones that seem determined to stay stuck in "process mode." They say things like, "What if we order flowers and someone is allergic to them? What if the vase drips water and someone slips on the floor?" What if...blah, blah, blah...

"C'mon," I told my reluctant first impression team, "live on the edge! Go wild! Look at us—we're ordering flowers without any data! Listen, if you try the flowers and they *do* end up posing a problem, then GET RID OF THEM, but at least try. Take some action. Change some impressions."

Here's the thing: Improving perception is not difficult; it's *different*. And as that story shows, sometimes different is a bigger barrier than difficult. You see, we are so used to changing outcomes, so conditioned to *working* on outcomes, that pulling in the perception piece is like trying to speak a foreign language.

So It's NOT About Hiding Ugly Patients!

Quint called me into his office one day and said, "Liz, your privacy scores in the Emergency Department are terrible."

I looked him in the eye and said, "Well, don't expect me to do anything about it."

As you might expect, Quint was surprised. He fired back with, "Excuse me?"

I explained, "Quint, we're seeing 48,000 patients in a room that's designed to see about 22,000. We've got these flimsy curtains around our carts; we've got people up and down the hallways peeking into rooms, looking at everything. If you're that concerned about privacy in our ER, you need to build a new Emergency Department."

Quint snapped, "We are NOT building a new ER."

"Well, what exactly do you expect me to do about privacy down there?" I demanded. (After all, I am not a miracle worker!)

"I don't know, Liz," Quint said. "It's your department; why don't you figure it out?"

Grrrrr! I went back to my office and started complaining to my old buddy, Don Dean. After listening to me rant and rave for a few minutes, Don stopped me and said, "Liz, when you pull a curtain around a patient's stretcher, do you let them know you're doing it for their privacy?"

"Well, DUH, DON!" It's a fair assumption that I wasn't even trying to hide my eye-rolls at this point. "Why else would we pull curtains around stretchers?"

"I'm just saying that your patients aren't mind readers. *They* might not know why you're pulling those curtains," Don said. "Can't hurt to explain it to them."

So, our Emergency Department gave Don's advice a try. (We were desperate, remember?) When we went into a patient's room, we said, "Now, Mrs. Smith, because we're concerned about your privacy while you're here with us in the ER, we're going to keep this curtain pulled around your stretcher."

Guess what happened to the privacy scores? They went up! We didn't have to hire one more FTE. We didn't have to build a $15 million ER. We didn't have to change the way we were working. (After all, we'd been pulling curtains for years!) All we had to do was *explain* what we were doing to our patients. Before Don's curtain revelation, no one in the ER had worried about our patients' perceptions, because we had the correct outcomes. Call in the Board of Health! Call in JCAHO! We are in full compliance!

It turns out that before we started explaining the reasoning behind curtain pulling, many of our patients had gotten the *wrong* impression. Most of them said, "Oh, I just figured you were pulling that curtain because you didn't want to look at me!"

OH, NO…it would *never* be that. (Wink, wink.)

The Easiest Thing in the World

Again, changing perception is not a difficult thing, but it *is* different. My team asked me, "Why can't these people figure it out themselves?!? Why do we have to tell these patients why we are pulling their curtains?"

I replied, "Why not?" It was the easiest of things to do. I mean, seriously—if a little narration is all it takes to make people's perceptions perk up, why wouldn't we narrate away?

It takes so little effort on our part. We don't have to change the way we work, we don't have to change our facility, and we don't have to change what happens in other people's departments. All we need to do is work with our patients and our customers to improve their perceptions and impressions of their care.

The (Unscientific) Truth About Quietness

If you still are not convinced that improving perception can be incredibly easy—and nearly instantaneous to achieve—here is one last story. I was working with a hospital that was struggling to improve its ratings on a particular question: "How often is your hospital quiet at night?" I am telling you, the hospital staff was actually mad at the patients. I met with a team who told me, "We have proof that the survey results are wrong!"

I said, "Really?" (I mean, this could be breaking news.) "Tell me more," I implored.

"Well, we score in the lowest group for that question," came the response. "So we formed a committee to study it…" *Rut-roh. Committees rarely get it right.* "…and one of the team members was our leader of Engineering…" *Hmm, sounds like a scientist…just sayin'!* "…so he rented a decibel meter reader. And he gathered data for over a month."

Every night, it turns out, this committee would do readings on the nursing units. Different units, different dates, different times of the night. And in over 100 readings, not *one* was over 60.

"See! There's the proof!" The spokesperson concluded. "The patients are wrong. WE ARE NOT A NOISY HOSPITAL!" *Whoa…right now you kinda are.*

I smiled at the team and said, "You did a quality measure. Decibel readings are an outcome. The problem is, your patients *perceive* the hospital to be noisy at night, even if it actually isn't.

The truth is, your patients probably aren't getting as much rest as they would like, and they're looking for something to blame it on.

"Now the way I see it, you have two choices. You could start a massive patient education campaign; you know, start telling people right on admission, 'This is *not* a noisy hospital at night, and we have the decibel reading to prove it!' ...Or you could try lowering your lights."

"Lower the lights!" the scientists exclaimed. "We are talking about noise, not brightness!"

"Yes," I said, striving for patience. "I understand. But right now, you turn down the hallway lights on the patient care units between 11 p.m. and 12 a.m. That makes sense; it's a traditional change-of-shift time. However, a lot of people try to go to sleep before midnight. So from now on, why don't you try lowering them around 8 p.m. after most of the visitors leave?"

The most scientific people in the room started to tremble. But miracle of miracles, they actually took my advice. After three months, guess what happened? Yep! When the lights were lowered around 8 p.m., the patients' perception was that the unit was quieter. Does it make scientific sense? No. Does it work? YES.

Now do you believe me? Okay then, one more chapter before I start sharing my strategies.

3

Myths About Perception Improvement (and a Few Excuses, Too)

You know me, I'm not afraid to call a spade a spade. So before we start talking strategy, let's touch on the myths—or, let's be real, *excuses*—people like to trot out when they're struggling to improve perception.

I have been helping organizations improve service excellence since the mid-1990s, and, believe me, I have heard just about every excuse in the world regarding why improving service is "impossible." (Heck, at various times in my career, I probably invented some of them.)

Because excuses can be some of the biggest roadblocks to change, I don't want you to read the upcoming chapters in this book with bogus beliefs floating around in your head. So let's debunk a few of the most common myths about perception before we go further.

The good news is we examined one of the biggest myths of all—the illusion that you can improve service by improving quality—in the last chapter. The bad news is there are a few more that need debunking. So let's move on.

Myth Number One: "We Don't Have the Time."

This one cracks me up because people are so serious about it. When they look at me, I can tell by their earnest, yet harried, facial expressions that they *really* believe they don't have the extra minutes to make a noticeable change in service perception.

As I've said before, changing perception is not about doing *more*; it's about doing things *differently*. Remember the curtain story from the previous chapter? It didn't take those of us in the ED any more time to say, "We are pulling this curtain for your privacy"—no, not one extra second. That's because (now get this!) we could actually say the words while we pulled the curtain. I know! Like walking and chewing gum.

Maybe you're still not convinced, so let me share my all-time favorite story about why you don't need more time to improve perception. When this story took place, I was doing work with an Emergency Department in a very small hospital.

As usual, I started off simply (or at least I thought it was pretty simple). I suggested to the team that they say to a patient upon arrival, "Hi! My name is Liz; I'm your nurse today.

It's important to me that you have a great visit. Please let me know if there's anything I can do."

Practically as one, the group looked at me with frowns and narrowed eyes. Their "spokesperson" (in other words, Ms. Bossy Pants) snorted, stood up, put her finger right in my face, and said, "Do you have any idea how busy we are?"

I'm thinking, *Yeah, the answer would be NOT busy! Are you kidding me?*

At 9,000 patients a year, I figured the ED in question saw approximately 24 patients a day. That's about one patient an hour. And yes, I know patients don't come through an Emergency Room's doors at equally spaced intervals. Still, it only takes about eight seconds to speak the "Hi! My name is Liz, blah, blah…" wording I'd given this group.

I'm no mathematical genius, but I felt pretty sure that even if all 24 patients this ED could expect to see in an average day came in at the same time, devoting eight extra seconds to each person was still very doable!

"Eight seconds to change a patient's perception…that sounds like a good deal to me!" I said. "And I promise you, those few extra seconds will pay off. Anyway," I added, "I know from personal experience that it takes about four seconds to say, 'Wow, are we busy today!' So, here's the deal: Complain less and you can save up those extra seconds to really make a difference."

It took a little convincing (and no, the entire team didn't adopt this practice at once), but a few brave people agreed to try my strategy. And lo and behold, they began to see results. I wasn't with this group long enough to find out if the rest of the team got on board, or if the eight seconds became too much to bear.

Myth Number Two: "We Don't Have the Resources."

We often think the best way (or the only way!) to improve a situation is to spend a lot of money and/or do a lot of work. That's definitely not true here. Improving perception doesn't take much money *or* effort. (I know, I know; I am sounding like a broken record. But let me say it again: This isn't about doing more; it is about doing things differently.)

Several years ago my mother was in the hospital. She was critically ill. She had a ruptured cerebral aneurysm, was on a ventilator, and in a coma. Initially the entire family gathered each day to visit, but after the first week, we started to take turns.

The first day I visited Mom on my own, I arrived early in the morning. Speaking to people in comas has proven to be very beneficial, so I began talking to my mother immediately. I read her the newspaper, I prayed out loud, I talked some more. (If you know me, you know that I can talk. My dear sister, Donna, says I can talk a dog off the meat wagon. Ha-ha, thanks, Sis.) After a while, though, I got tired of talking to myself, so I went down to the cafeteria and bought a tuna sandwich and a Diet Coke, which I brought back up to my mother's room. Then I proceeded to click on the TV and make myself comfortable in the room's nice big chair, borrowing the bedside table for my lunch.

As I was opening that Diet Coke, a tech walked by and caught me, eyeball to eyeball, just as the can went "whoosh!" *Oh man…I am busted!* I thought to myself. *There is probably some rule about having tuna in the ICU.*

Not 15 seconds later, though, that very same tech walked in with a tall Styrofoam cup filled with ice. "I thought you might like this for your soda," she said as she handed it to me.

Wow! I was blown away. In that moment, this tech was my hero. I mean no offense to the neurosurgeon or to the great team of nurses in that ICU, of course, but at that particular moment, that technician was my hero!

Here's the point of my story: This woman's actions took almost zero resources. As I've stated, her detour into Mom's room didn't take more than 15 seconds. That cup full of ice didn't cost the hospital more than a few pennies. And the tech herself didn't have to sift through piles of policy manuals to determine how to respond to "daughter has a Diet Coke…" but with that simple gesture, she still made a huge difference to me.

No matter your field or industry, one thing will be true for most of your organization's perception-boosting actions: They probably won't require much expense or time or knowledge, but simply thoughtfulness.

Myth Number Three: "Only Crabby People Fill Out Surveys."

Once upon a time at Holy Cross Hospital… (Sorry, but I always think that's how those HCH stories should begin!) Anyway…once upon a time at Holy Cross Hospital, we reached the 94th percentile of service excellence after a year of work. Quint, as he has become famous for, immediately raised the bar. Our goal for the following year was the 99th percentile. Quint *could* have been happy with 94th, but noooooooooooooo! (I guess that's why he and the organizations that work with Studer Group are so successful.)

At the time this new goal was set, Don Dean and I were sharing an office. (No, I wasn't still in trouble—we actually discovered that we liked being roommates. It was fun to have someone to bounce ideas off of, and to help solve problems.)

Don was the hospital's measurement guru (and to this day he is still the best in the country!). Now, he had been given the task of getting the organization from the 94th percentile to the 99th percentile in one year. "We have to eliminate all of our 'very poors' and 'poors,'" he declared— meaning the patients who rated us a one or two on the measurement tool we were using.

"That's impossible," I answered. C'mon. I had been working with patients, families, and visitors for over 15 years, and I knew for a fact that you can't *eliminate* all the people who might be upset with you. In fact, sometimes, pleasing those extremely difficult people will have an adverse effect on the folks who think you are doing a great job.

"We have to, Liz," Don responded. "How else will we get to the 99th?"

"I don't know, but you are the Duke of Data…I am sure you will figure out the answer. I mean, if you just look, or review…" I trailed off.

"You're right, you're right, you're right," Don replied. Now, don't think he was all that enthusiastic about my comments. After sharing an office with me for a couple of years, Don had simply learned that if he said, "You're right," three times in a row, I would stop talking. Kind of the reverse of Beetlejuice: Say his name three times, he appears; say, "You're right," three times and Liz disappears—or at least shuts up.

A few days later, Don sat down across from me with a big smile on his face. "I figured it out. We do not have to move the patients who think we are 'poor' or 'very poor.' The path to the 99th percentile is moving the people who think we are 'good' to 'very good.'"

The Master of Measurement had just earned his title. Although you may have heard about this wonderful strategy before, I promise you it is because Mr. Dean uncovered it over 20 years ago.

Now, I am not a measurement guru, but I can look at data and figure things out. Because of my time learning from Don, though, there are two things I can say with absolute certainty: Plenty of people who are *not* crabby fill out surveys. And fixating solely on unhappy customers/patients is not the way to improve your overall service measures.

Believe it or not, even in the worst of the worst organizations in healthcare, less than 10 percent of patients rank them as being "very poor." It doesn't matter which survey you look at or what type of scale is being used (e.g., 1-4, 1-10, etc.). It doesn't matter what you call that lowest rating (e.g., never, very poor, very dissatisfied, etc). And it doesn't matter if you are looking at Inpatient, ED, Home Health, or another department. You simply will not find even the poorest-performing organization being ranked at the bottom of the scale by more than 10 percent of its respondents.

For instance, take a look at this comparison. This graphic shows the Inpatient scores of two hospitals, one of which scored in the 90th percentile, the other in the lower 10th.

Percentile Rank	10th	92nd
Very Poor	3.2	1.0
Poor	4.0	1.3
Fair	13.5	5.4
Good	38.5	30.4
Very Good	40.9	61.7

Notice that the difference between the lowest scores for each organization is only about 2 points. Again, that is between an organization in the 10th percentile (i.e., really poor performance) and the 92nd percentile (outstanding performance). You can see that as the scores go up, the gaps between the two organizations become greater, resulting in a monumental 20-point difference in the Very Good category.

So, I think we can agree that crabby and unhappy people are *not* the only ones filling out surveys. While respondents at the highly rated organization were (understandably) more satisfied with their experience overall, the vast majority of respondents from the low-ranked organization were still satisfied.

This pattern repeats itself over and over again. Don't believe me? Go look at your own organization's results. I think you will be surprised by how few people are ranking you very poorly. I promise you it is less than 10 percent.

Here's something that may surprise you: The techniques and strategies that I will share with you in this book will not move your unhappy people. Let's face it: Those 10 percenters (that's what I call crabby people) are difficult to move. Some of them have legitimate concerns, but many others just *don't want* to change their opinions. They're determined to be dissatisfied.

Here's the good news: I know how to move the middle group of respondents to "very good" territory. Look at the previous example. If we moved half of the "fairs," and about a quarter of the "goods," we could move that low-ranked organization from the basement to the penthouse! So as you read this book, do your best to forget the 10 percenters. Focus your efforts on moving the perceptions of those folks in the middle.

Myth Number Four: "That Doesn't Always Work."

But this doesn't work on everyone. That phrase really gets under my skin! Yes, I know very well that there is not a tactic out there that works for every patient, all the time. I know that the practices I teach will most likely *not* work on your 10 percenters…but guess what? That means they *will* work the other **90 percent** of the time.

HELLO! How crazy is it that most of us stop when something doesn't work a full 100 percent of the time? That's right—pretty crazy. But the thing is, if something is crazy, I have probably done it at one point or another. Yep.

I remember that when I was in the middle of my "brat" phase, I was sent to a class on patient satisfaction. We students were instructed to say "hi" to everyone we met in the hallways, waiting rooms, or units.

Begrudgingly, I gave "hi" a whirl. Walking back from the class, I said hello to people in the corridors, whether they were colleagues or visitors. Things were going well. People smiled back and greeted me, too. As I approached the Emergency Department, I said hi to the police officers and firefighters in the lobby. I nodded and said hello to people walking in and out of the waiting room. As I moved into the ED, I was really getting into the swing of things. I said hi to a patient sitting in a wheelchair, and then I turned the corner and said hello to a man on a stretcher.

That's when things fell apart. This man looked at me and shouted, "FUDGE YOU!" (But he didn't actually say "fudge," if ya know what I mean. Looking back, I suppose this patient's restraints and disheveled look should have been a clue that he might not respond cheerfully.) In any case, that was it. That was all the proof I needed in order to declare that saying hi didn't work!

I'll be honest. I was looking for a reason to stop. Do you remember my story in the Introduction about my team being upset about saying hi? Well, rewind a couple years back, and I was just the same. I was looking for a reason to resist. I was happy to be finished with greeting other people, because I hadn't been gung-ho about that class to begin with. I was done with that hello stuff less than 30 minutes after leaving the class. Even though I'd said hi to at least nine people with great results, number 10 (there's that 10 percenter!) is the reason I quit. And if you'd asked me back then, I would have been adamant that I was correct in deciding that the idea of saying hi just didn't work.

Trust me. All of the things I talk about in the following chapters will work. Really, I promise! But they won't work 100 percent of the time. So please, please, PLEASE don't give up when you encounter a 10 percenter. A 90 percent success rate still makes a very big difference. You will see great results, and most importantly, so will all those folks in the middle who will appreciate your efforts.

Okay. Ready? Here we go!

4

SAY WHAT?!? Make Your Words Work

Words are *the* key when creating great impressions. Yes, I know we've been taught that actions speak louder than words, but the truth is, when creating great experiences, we need both. And too often, our actions can be misinterpreted on their own. (Remember the curtain story?) So as we interact with customers and patients, words become even more important.

I realize that the words we use with the people we serve can be a sensitive subject. But before we get into the debate about being "scripted" versus being a "robot," let me share one of my favorite stories.

Welcome Home—to the Peabody!

One of my all-time favorite hotels is the Peabody in Memphis, Tennessee. It is a very old, very charming hotel with an elegant and spacious lobby. The best part about the Peabody's lobby is the big, beautiful fountain in the middle. Why? The fountain has ducks swimming in it. *I know.* How cool is that? But that's not all. Every day at 11 a.m., the ducks waddle down a red carpet to the fountain in a little parade, complete with marching band music. (Okay, I know. Right now you are thinking, *Get a life!* But hey, I am on the road almost 20 days a month. Those ducks make me happy!)

The last time I went to the Peabody, I got out of the car and the bellboy said to me, "Hello. How's your day?"

"Things are going well," I told him.

He asked, "Is this your first visit to the Peabody?"

I shook my head. "Oh no, I've been here before."

"Well then, welcome home!" he smiled.

Awww, I thought to myself.

Okay now, let's analyze this. Mentally, I knew that the bellboy wasn't all that excited to see me. And as much as I love the Peabody Hotel, I know the Peabody Hotel in Memphis, Tennessee, is *not* my home. However, emotionally (here's where perception comes in!), I felt all warm and fuzzy when that kid said, "Welcome home." (I bet you would have too.) Those words gave me the impression of comfort we all get when we find ourselves in familiar surroundings.

Now, I do this for a living. That kid was scripted, okay? During his orientation in some basement room of that hotel, he was told, "When people come here, ask them if they've been to the Peabody before. If they say no, say, 'Welcome to the Peabody.' If they say yes, say, 'Welcome home.'" Bada-bing, bada-boom, done!

But you know what? That script worked. It put me in a better mood, and I guarantee that I was a nicer person when I walked into the lobby and saw three people ahead of me in line for check-in. And at no time did I feel as though that bellboy was a robot! He didn't seem like a "Stepford" boy. He wasn't an automaton or a talking manikin. In fact, it was the opposite. To me, he seemed warm and friendly, almost charming.

The Good Word on Scripts: They Aren't the Bad Guy!

Here's the point of my Peabody story: Please, please, PLEASE don't get turned off of scripts. I promise you they are not a bad thing. Yes, I know some people hate the thought of them. I know that many organizations won't even allow the word "script" to be used officially, so they have come up with better words (which is great, really, because that is what this chapter is all about!). So whether you call them key words, strategic sayings, word tools, or quintessential questions, it's okay; they all work.

> I love the creativity of some organizations. One group I was working with said to me, "It insults us professionally to call them 'scripts,' so we use 'fabulous phrases!'" Oh, my stars…what is that? I cannot believe that any team out there, except maybe the Rockettes, would use the term "fabulous phrases" in the workplace.

Despite all the options, I still call them scripts because I am old school, and I'm just keeping it real. A script is a script no matter what it is called, and deep down, you and your colleagues know it.

I don't know why we hate scripts so much. Think about it: Scripts help us to do our jobs well. They make sure that we remember to dot all of our i's and cross all of our t's. Almost all of us have been scripted at some point in our careers. Educators are scripted—think lesson plans. Realtors use scripts—ever heard "charming fixer-upper"? Receptionists use them too—"It is my pleasure to connect you." And clergy *for sure* use scripts—scripture and liturgies! Heck, anyone who records their outgoing voicemail message has used a script. They are everywhere.

For the clinicians out there, think about when you learned to take a health history. You were scripted to start by asking the patient questions about his head on down to his toes. Those questions were part of a script. Did anyone say, "I'm not going from the head to the toes. That insults me professionally. Instead, I'm going to start on the right and work my way left!" Of course not, because time and experience show everyone that starting from the head and working your way to the toes is the best way to get an accurate history.

Face it. You already use scripts yourself. Don't you hear yourself saying the same thing over and over again every day?

Scripts: What *Not* to Do

Here's why I think so many people have a problem with scripts: Most of the scripts that we contrive do *not* do a great job of improving perceptions.

The dentist who says, "Now this won't hurt a bit" is using a bad script because it is a LIE! Ever hear a nurse say, "You'll feel a little mosquito bite" when preparing an IV? Yeah, that's a bad script too, because a needle is *not* a mosquito. And the math teacher who tells the class that algebra is fun is a big ol' fibber as well.

As always, I am guilty of using bad scripts myself. I once concocted a script that I routinely used when discharging patients from the Emergency Department at Holy Cross. Whether they were being admitted upstairs or going home, the last thing that I said to them was, "Good luck to you."

I meant it in the nicest way possible. (No really, I did!) But that is not the best script, is it? Of course not. Think about it. You are being admitted up to 4West and the last thing the ED nurse says is, "Now we are going to transfer you up to 4West. Good luck to you." YIKES! You're probably thinking, *Where are they sending me that this nurse is basically saying, "Fingers crossed, you'll do okay"?!?*

Or imagine this: You are being sent home after spraining your ankle and the ortho tech says, "Now remember, the doctor wants you to use crutches for the next 10 days. Good luck to you." Wow. Once again, that does not inspire confidence.

The long and short of this story is, I had to change my discharge script. Once I realized how *not* reassuring it was, I switched to the phrase, "Thank you for putting your trust in us today." Guess what? That took the exact same amount of time, but left a totally different perception.

Words Are Important.

Words are critical because of their impact on perception. Certain words and phrases can instantly make our customers or patients feel more comfortable or less anxious—but only if we use them wisely.

Think about the word "care." Most people use it to indicate that they had a good experience. For instance, if you say, "The staff cared about me," you probably mean that the staff was thoughtful and kind, and that they paid special attention to you.

But in healthcare that word is used differently, isn't it? Clinicians use the word "care" to describe treatment or therapeutic intervention, or sometimes diagnostic procedures. For example, you might hear questions like, "Is there enough staff to perform patient *care* activities today?" Or, "What's the patient's *care* plan?" There is nothing wrong with that.

However, patients and customers need to be able to hear us use "care" in a different way—for instance, "Did the staff care about you?"

"Did the Staff Care About You?": A Case Study

When I work with organizations, I teach people how to use the word "care" so that it can make a positive perception difference. To show you what I mean, let's use an outpatient example.

A patient goes to a facility to have some x-rays and lab work done. Upon arrival he walks up to the information desk and hands the greeter his written orders. The person who takes them says, "Welcome, Mr. Smith. We've been expecting you today. Please have a seat in our waiting area, and a registration clerk will call you. I care that you're comfortable while you're waiting, so please let me know if there's anything I can do for you."

At registration, the clerk says, "I care that when you get home today, you're not spending three hours on the phone with your insurance company. So, we're going to take your information down as accurately as possible."

A bit later, the lab technician says, "I care that you are comfortable with this procedure. Do you have any questions, and do you have a preferred site for me to perform the blood draw?" Next, the x-ray tech says, "We're going to take really good care of you today while we are getting these pictures. Please let us know if there is anything you need."

What do you think that patient's perception is going to be when asked the question, "Did the staff care about you?" Unless he is one of those incorrigible 10-percenters, the answer is going to be, "Yes!"

Guess what? Getting similar results in your own organization won't take any extra time or effort. None of those example phrases I used above takes more than eight seconds to say. All you have to do is commit to saying them.

Remember, your words are important. They can change impressions. They can improve perceptions.

Key Words, in Your Own Words

If your organization hasn't chosen any key words to use in your perception-improving scripts (like "care"), or if you are struggling with service in general, relax. You don't have to come up with a whole bunch of new happy words or "fabulous phrases." All you have to do is be observant.

First, talk to the people you serve. They will let you know what's important to them if you ask! You can also review comments you receive in writing and verbally. You can read your evaluations and look for both the good and bad comments. You can check out social media and see what people are saying out there in cyberspace.

Key words are easy to identify if you ask the most important people—the people you serve—what's meaningful to them.

That said, some things are universal when it comes to creating great customer experiences with excellent impressions and perceptions. Most people look for courtesy and respect. They want us to listen to them and take their concerns seriously. They want to be treated like an individual—not a number— and they want to stay informed. Oh—and they need that information to be explained to them in a way that they can understand. Most importantly, people want to be treated with care and kindness.

So let's break this down. First up is courtesy and respect. If I were trying to improve those perceptions, I might ask my team to use the phrase, "I want to make sure you feel as though we respect your wishes today, so please let me know if there's anything I can do for you."

If I were working on making sure that someone's individual needs were met, I might include this statement when talking to the customer or patient: "We care that you have everything you need to have a great day, so please let us know if you have any special requests."

When sharing knowledge, rather than using words like "tell," "review," or "inform," I would use the word "explain." So: "Let me explain the tests you are scheduled to have tomorrow" instead of "I am going to tell you about your tests."

Be *especially* careful to use words that your customer or patient can relate to. I once worked with a team that struggled to help patients understand their discharge instructions. We tried implementing all kinds of strategies. We changed to computerized instructions. We asked our patients to repeat their instructions, but nothing worked. It wasn't until we stopped calling them "discharge instructions" that we saw an improvement.

Yep! When we switched from "Let me explain your discharge instructions" to "Let me explain your home care instructions," the patient's perception changed immediately. Home care instructions were something they could understand. But discharge instructions, well, when you think about it, sounds like you are dealing with a creepy disease, huh?

Phony? Who Cares?

If we do the things I've mentioned above—treat people with respect, listen to their needs, and explain things in a way they can understand—then 90 percent of the time they are going to feel that they are being treated with care and kindness.

Yet, I still get the big pushback that scripting is too phony. Or similarly, "What if the customers or patients know we are scripted?" To that I say, "Who cares?" Scripting didn't bother me at the Peabody. And I honestly don't think it matters anywhere.

> Even when people know we are using scripts, they are still very effective because at the very least, they demonstrate that the organization is concerned about you, regardless of what the individual employee might be thinking.

Are you ready for another story? I was at Logan Airport in Boston, and my flight was delayed by two hours. (I know, shocker!) So I went in search of food and found that the famous Boston restaurant Legal Seafood had an eatery in the terminal. I sat down, and when the waiter came up, he started with some pretty basic words: "Hi, my name is Dan, and I'll be your server today." But then he added two amazing questions: "How are you fixed for time today?" and "Do you have any food allergies that I should be aware of?"

Brilliant! In asking me those questions, the waiter hit so many of the important satisfiers. He was respectful of my time, he showed courtesy in his introduction, he took my concerns seriously, he listened to my needs, and he treated me as an individual. He was asking me about the things that were important to me as an air traveler (time) and as a diner (allergies). Overall, Dan the Waiter made me feel that he was extremely concerned about me as an individual. Who cares if he was *told* to ask those questions? They worked! So simple, but brilliant.

Ask Not How You Can Make Your Job Easier; Ask What You Can Do for the Customer.

One of the most effective key phrases I know involves simply asking people, "Is there anything else I can do for you?" This hits on so many levels because it demonstrates care, concern, respect, courtesy, and thoughtfulness. It is truly effective...and it is also the one phrase that staff tends to hate the most.

Oh man, when I talk about this in a presentation, people see red. Some people heckle me: "Do you know how busy we are here? Do you think anyone in their right mind is going to say to patients, 'Is there anything else I can do for you? I'm a little bored!' Or, 'Is there anything else I can do for you? I was hoping you could dream up some stuff for me to do today.' Or, 'Is there anything else I can do for you? Perhaps I can shove a broom up my butt and sweep the floor as I leave the room.'"

Yes, I have heard them all. And I am also here to tell you that when you ask people if there is anything else you can do for them, they don't make stuff up! They ask you for the same thing they're going to ask you for anyway, except when you're down the hall, already tied up with another patient, already busy on a phone call, or assisting a coworker.

Asking people what they need doesn't make you busier, but it *does* make a huge difference in perception. If 10 people a shift ask a patient, "Is there anything else I can do for you?" and the patient has a request only two of those times, that means eight times a shift the patient is answering, "No, I'm good. Everything is fine." Do you think that makes a difference in perception? YES.

When you've got a whole organization asking this question, it makes life better for everyone. If you're the last person in the room and you say, "Is there anything else I can do for you? Do you have any other questions?" you've just made life better for the next person who walks in. Over time, paying it forward like this has a snowball effect. Everyone's job is easier, and overall satisfaction is improved.

Please don't resist using scripting, key words, word tools, or whatever you call them. The right words can enhance impressions, improve perceptions, and most importantly, create better experiences. This is not about chasing scores or "working" the survey; it's about improving the customer's or patient's experience. And it works!

5

Tell the Truth...with a Little Cushion (The Art of Expectations Management)

We all know that the best service organizations are masters at exceeding customers' expectations. We've been told to do the same thing ourselves. But what most of us don't know is that in order to *exceed* expectations, you must *manage* them first.

Let's start with a simple example. You go to a restaurant, where the hostess tells you the wait for a table is 30 minutes. But after 40 minutes, you still haven't been seated. Are you getting ticked? Oh yeah, I know *I'm* getting ticked. And when I'm finally seated after 45 minutes, I am downright grumpy.

Now, let's say that the next time you go out to eat, you're told that you'll have to wait an hour. When you get a table after 45 minutes, are you happy? Of course! (Unless, of course, you're some weirdo who looks at the clock and says to the hostess,

"I'm not sitting now. I have 15 more minutes to stand here in this lobby!") What was the difference in wait time between these two examples? None! The difference was how your expectations were managed.

Here's the lesson: Organizations that excel in customer service have learned how to set expectations they know they can exceed. It's not that they have reduced wait times; it's not that they are perfect; and they definitely haven't eradicated annoyances. They have simply learned how to manage people's expectations.

Nobody Likes to Be Ignored.

Many of us have made a big mistake when it comes to understanding human nature. We think people are intolerant of inconvenience or waiting. They're not. You know what human beings are intolerant of? *Being ignored.*

Human beings have very, very little tolerance for being ignored. Read that line again. It is very important!

Let's go back to the restaurant example. When you were told that the wait was 30 minutes but you had to sit in the lobby for 45, why were you so angry? It wasn't because you were waiting. I'm betting your blood pressure rose because for those last 15 minutes, you felt *ignored.* As soon as a half-hour passed, you started looking around to make sure no one who came in after you was seated first, didn't you? (Admit it!) You assumed that if anyone else got seated ahead of you, then you surely must have been forgotten. (In this situation, I'd personally move closer to the hostess just to be sure she could still see me, and so that she could see that I was not happy!)

When you were told the wait time was an hour, though, you didn't worry about anyone skipping ahead of you in line after 30 minutes had passed. You didn't assume that you had been forgotten because your expectations were managed.

Busting the Unwritten Rule:
NEVER Give a Time Estimate!

Okay, bear with me on this restaurant example just a little longer. I think that both restaurants knew that they had a 45-minute wait time. The restaurant manager who understood customer satisfaction told her employees, "Tell them the wait will be an hour, and if we seat them in 45, 50, or even 55 minutes, they're still going to be happy."

However, the other restaurant was probably run by someone who used to be in healthcare. Why do I say that? Because in healthcare, we think that if we don't tell people how long they'll have to wait, they won't notice how much time is passing. (Yeah, right.)

I'm serious: How many professionals do you know who give out time estimates? I'm guessing not many. In fact, most of us have created a set of phrases to mask that information. Although experience has taught us *about* how long the wait time will be, or how long a procedure will take, we still resist giving out actual minutes or hours. It's like an unwritten rule for many of us: *Never give them a time estimate.*

Here's how the time-dodge dance goes:
Someone asks, "How long will this take?"

You reply, "Oh, that's going to be a bit."

"A bit? How long is a bit?"

"Hmm," you stall. "Shorter than a while, longer than pretty soon. It's about the same as 'not too bad.'" …
What kind of craziness is that?!?

Tell Them What You Know… with a Little Cushion.

"We can't give out times in healthcare, because how can we possibly know how long things will take?" you protest. "When we're in the ER, we don't know how busy it's going to get. When we're in the OR, we don't know how long a case is going to take. And if the issue is an IT problem, we don't know how long the system will be down. You can't tell a person what you don't know!"

I'll bet there are people in education who say something very similar: "We can't put a time on how long a counseling session might take; every student is an individual." And so on and so forth, throughout every industry.

Yeah, I don't buy it. I'll admit that unless you're a psychic, you'll never be able to *exactly* predict how long every task and procedure will take. But I believe that 85 percent of the time, you still have a pretty good idea.

If you've worked in your department for over a year, you know how things work. You know that on the days when big ortho clinics are scheduled, x-rays tend to get backed up. You know which days the system tends to be the busiest. You know the parents who talk the most. You know when the hospital is full, meaning that *everything* takes longer to accomplish. You know which days you're scheduled to work with "Joe Slow." Don't you? See, no matter where you work, you KNOW...yes, you know.

And guess what? You don't *have* to know exactly how long something will take to effectively manage expectations. All you need is a ballpark estimate, which your experience can tell you. Take that number, give yourself some cushion, and then pass your estimate on to the customer. It's really that simple.

Remember, organizations that excel in service set expectations that they know they can exceed. Human beings don't like to be ignored. Too often we think that if there is a wait, inconvenience, or hassle, it is better not to tell the customer or patient. I am here to tell you, that doesn't work!

Disney may have started it. At each ride they have those little signs that read, "The wait from this point forward is 30 minutes." You read that, and it's like, *Whew*! They really move those lines fast, too, because it usually takes only 24 or 25 minutes before you're stepping onto the ride. Disney sets expectations that they know they can exceed. I read recently that someone thought Disney's system must be wrong because the sign read 50 minutes and they waited only 20. I don't think that was an error. I believe it is Disney's way of managing expectations.

Come Fly with Me.

I fly a lot. Let's say it is a Friday and we are in Columbus, Ohio (a city not all that far from Chicago, and—let's face it—with airport delays, sometimes I think I could walk home faster). Anyway, you and I get on the plane, they shut the door, and they pull us out on that tarmac. And then it happens: You hear the sad (so sad!) sound of the engines shutting down...and now you know you're trapped like a rat.

Over the intercom, you hear the pilot announce, "Ladies and gentlemen, I've got some bad news. We've just been told by the tower that O'Hare is on a 30-minute ground hold."

Oh! I'm never happy to hear that, but I'm happier to hear that than to hear nothing at all. It doesn't happen that much anymore, but if I'm on that plane, stuck on the tarmac with the engines shut down, and I've been told *nothing*, I get angry. I feel ignored because I've been sitting there for 20 minutes and no one has told me why we're not up in the air. Yeah, I'm ticked.

At that point, I'm going to get aggravated at the first person I see. Usually, that's the flight attendant. Right? But in reality the flight attendant and the pilot really have nothing to do with the delay. It's not their fault. But that's who we blame unless we are told more about the holdup. Again, if I am told about the wait, I might not be happy, but I am not getting ticked off at the wrong people, either.

Now, every once in a while you get a pilot who understands exceeding expectations. He'll get on the intercom after being told there's a 30-minute hold and say, "Ladies and gentlemen, I've got some bad news. I've just been told we're on a *45-minute* ground hold but I'm going to see what I can do to get us pushed up ahead of the pack."

He gets back on the intercom in 30 minutes and says, "Ladies and gentlemen, good news! I just got us cleared for takeoff and we're heading out to the runway. We're number two in line."

People on the plane start clapping. Don't they? It's the *exact same* wait time. What's different is how our expectations were managed.

Oh, I can hear some of you right now. You're saying, "That's not fair; it's cheating!"

No, it is not cheating, because that is exactly how most people want their expectations managed. Tell me the wait in the restaurant is an hour and seat me in 45 minutes, and I'm happier. Tell me the delay on the flight is 45 minutes and get me in the air in 30 minutes, and I'm happier. That's human nature. We're not cheating when we do that with the people we serve.

Who Comes up with Their Own Expectations, Anyway?

Another mistake we tend to make (in addition to believing people can't handle waiting) is assuming that if we don't set the expectation for the customer, they won't have one. WRONG! When we don't set expectations, people set their own. And guess what? When that happens, they set expectations that we can't possibly meet, much less exceed. And that, my friends, is a recipe for failure.

Here's an internal customer example. Let's say I'm the manager of the ICU and I enter an order into the system for an item I'm going to need. Then I call down to Purchasing to let them know the urgency. They say, "Okay, we'll get it to you as soon as we can."

I'm thinking to myself, *There are big delivery trucks that come to this hospital every day, so how long could this delivery possibly take…two days? Seems reasonable to me.* So when the item I ordered hasn't arrived after three days, I'm annoyed. And when it finally shows up in four days, I am downright angry.

What would happen, though, if Purchasing tells me what to expect? What if I'm told, "Okay, Liz, normally it takes us four or five days to get this particular item in, but we'll do our best to get it sooner if we can." When that item shows up on the fourth day, I'm happy.

Here's another example involving a patient. Let's say you go into a patient's room to draw some blood. "We'll get the results back for you quickly," you say. The patient, who isn't a medical professional, thinks, *They took only one tube of blood. I watch medical TV shows. This is only going to take maybe 20 or 30 minutes, max.*

You guessed it: The blood work is *not* back in 30 minutes, and the patient is starting to get annoyed. At 40 minutes, he hears people laughing at the nurse's station and gets more aggravated. At 50 minutes, the patient starts doing the head bob. (If you're in healthcare you know what I'm talking about: The patient starts poking his head out of the doorway every few minutes. Poke. Peek. Poke. Peek.) You know why? He set his own *incorrect* expectations about how long the blood work should take, and now that those bogus expectations haven't been met, he is feeling ignored. When you walk back into his room after an hour and 10 minutes, you've got an angry patient on your hands, and you, my friend, are the villain.

Here's what should have happened. Since it's not your first week on the job, you know that your lab results are usually back in an hour. So you say to the patient, "Now I am going to send your blood down to the lab. Normally, it takes an hour and a half for it to come back (*See what you just did there? You gave yourself a cushion!*), but we're going to see if we can't get yours back any sooner." When you return with the patient's results after "only" an hour and 10 minutes, you're a hero. Same exact wait time, but in this scenario, the difference is that *you* set and managed the patient's expectations.

You Know the Drill—But Most of Them Don't.

People who know the drill are easier—really, they are. Ask a flight attendant—they prefer the frequent flyer to the first-time rookie, because we FFs know what to expect. We don't freak out when we hit a bit of turbulence, we know exactly what size roller bag will fit in the overhead compartment, and we consider a 45-minute delay the same as being on time.

Likewise, educators know that the parents of five children tend to be more "chill" than the parents of only children. And if you are in healthcare, I know you have noticed that chronic patients are often "easier" than first-time patients. That's because chronic patients know what to expect. They aren't making incorrect assumptions.

For example, you can usually identify the family of a patient who has had multiple surgeries. They come to the surgical waiting room dressed in comfy clothes and armed with magazines, craft projects, and snacks. These families know the drill. After their loved one is wheeled into the OR, they check in with the volunteer, then head off to the cafeteria for breakfast. When they get back, they stake out their section of the waiting room. These aren't rookies…they know the very best spots—the ones close to the TV, bathrooms, and coffee.

These families also have accurate expectations regarding time. They do not approach the desk every 30 minutes. Their watches are all synchronized. When they were told that the procedure would take about 90 minutes, they automatically front loaded 60 minutes onto that estimate because they know from experience that there's always extra time between wheeling the patient into the OR and the beginning of the procedure. These folks also tacked a 45-minute buffer on the end of the operation, understanding that it takes time to move a patient from the OR to the recovery area. Add another 15 minutes for a little "this and that," and they are well prepared for a three-and-a-half-hour wait.

Of course, these been-there-done-that patients (and their families) are the exception. Most people come to us with unrealistic expectations. And that is where the danger lies. Fortunately, correcting and managing their unrealistic expectations is not all that difficult.

Let's say that the family in the example above are newbies instead of veterans. To keep them from losing their minds after 90 minutes, all you need to do is ask the surgeon and the nurse to explain the full timeline: "The procedure itself takes about 90 minutes; however, we need about an hour before and an hour after, so you should plan on three and a half hours of waiting time."

Be Honest, Even When the Truth Hurts.

Face it. Most of the time, patients and their families don't understand how long things (whatever those "things" may be!) can take. Or even worse, they presume to know how events "should" roll out, often basing their assumptions on what they've seen happen on TV. Most times, *of course*, they are way off base. That means there's absolutely nothing wrong—and a lot right!—with letting people know what's going to happen.

I think that often we keep our mouths shut because we know the patient won't like what we have to say. *If I don't deliver the bad news, maybe the patient won't realize how crummy this situation is!* you think. (It's similar to believing that people won't notice how long the wait is if we don't give them an estimate.)

I once worked with an outpatient pharmacy team who told me, "You know, Liz, normally we fill our scripts in 20 minutes. But when there's a big family practice clinic going on, it can sometimes take us up to two hours, and our techs are just afraid to tell people that."

WHAT?!? How insanely frustrated would *you* be if you were getting a prescription filled and you had to wait two hours for it? Don't you think it would be better to be told up front, "We're sorry, but it is taking us two and a half hours (*There's that cushion time!*) to fill prescriptions today."

I, for one, would much rather receive this information before sitting down in the waiting room. I might not be happy, but at least I would be able to make an informed decision: "Well, I'd better leave and come back later today," or, "I'll just come back tomorrow," or, "I'd better call somebody to pick up my kid from school because there's no way I'm making it there in time."

If we don't tell people what to expect, not only are we ignoring them, but we are depriving them of the ability to plan for the future. We are not giving them what they need to be happier customers and happier patients.

Managing expectations is an unfamiliar practice for most of us, but it is also one of the most effective ways to improve perception. When the people we serve feel as though they are in the know, they will be more satisfied. So, here's what you need to remember:

- Tell them what's going on and what they can expect.
- Explain things in a way people can understand.
- Tell the truth, even when it's not pleasant.

Always remember, when you manage expectations, you decrease anxiety. And most importantly, when *you* set the expectation, *you* can exceed the expectation. That is the formula for making a huge positive impact on the customer's or patient's perception!

6

"Yeah, We Know It Stinks!": How to Win Them Over by Acknowledging Inconvenience

Let's face it: None of us is perfect. Surprising, right? Seriously, though, despite our best efforts, everyday things happen that upset our patients, irritate families, and annoy customers. I'm talking about delays, problems, mistakes, etc. And because we know these things will happen, a lot of organizations rely on service recovery plans.

I do believe that all organizations need to have strong service recovery strategies in place. However, the first step in service recovery is the ability to acknowledge inconvenience. I always find it amusing when organizations spend a lot of time and money educating their teams on service recovery, but don't address acknowledging inconvenience. It is like teaching someone to run before they can walk.

A Tale of Two Checkouts

Admit it! We do inconvenient things to people *all the time*. What we don't do is address or acknowledge that inconvenience. As I explained earlier in this book, I don't think we have really wrapped our heads around how much it irritates people to believe that they are being ignored. On the flip side, though, I also don't think we understand how very tolerant people can become once we've acknowledged their inconvenience.

Not sure what it means to acknowledge inconvenience? Okay, picture this: You're in the grocery store after a long day at work. After you find all the items on your list, you make your way to the registers, only to spend more time standing in line than you did filling your whole basket. When you finally get up to the counter, the cashier is cranky. (In her defense, she has been working all day without a break, the store is busy, and she's been dealing with more than her fair share of "extreme couponers.")

By the time you are face-to-face with her, the cashier doesn't even try to hide her negative attitude. As she starts man-handling your eggs, squeezing your bread, and throwing your apples into a bag, you find yourself fighting the urge to lean across the counter and shout, "Listen! Easy on the groceries! And by the way, can I speak to your manager?" Not that the manager could help, because by this point, you've turned into one of those impossible-to-please 10 percenters…you know what I'm saying?

Now, what if your checkout experience had unfolded differently? When you get up to the register, the cashier looks at you and says, "I am so sorry that you had to wait in line so long today; I don't know why the store is so busy. We're not giving things away for free. Again, I'm really sorry you had to wait."

What do you say to her? Probably something like, "Oh, that's okay, honey!" AND you start helping her bag the groceries... don't you? Sure you do! "I'll take that, dear, and you just keep ringing. Oh—and let me get that heavy laundry soap in the bottom of the basket."

As soon as our inconvenience is acknowledged, we turn back into a 90 percenter. We realize that the cashier doesn't make out the grocery store work schedule and isn't responsible for the fact that only three of twelve lines are open. She doesn't manage the store. And she's been working the whole time we've been standing in line. She hasn't been flirting with the bag boy or chit-chatting with the girl at the next counter! Yes, when our inconvenience has been recognized, most of us turn into very understanding people.

But sometimes in the workplace, just like the cashier in the first scenario, we want people to figure out how busy we are. We want our customers and patients to feel sorry for us because we have been working sooooo hard.

Here's some news for you: That's not how most people are going to react, *especially* in a service industry! If we want our customers and patients to be "rational," understanding, and cut us some slack, we must be the first ones to extend the olive branch by recognizing *their* inconvenience. We need to say, in effect, "We know this stinks." Then, they'll have the perception that not only did we notice their annoyance or aggravation, we also cared enough to acknowledge it!

In the example above, which cashier do you think goes home in a better mood? The second one, of course! People have been helping her all day. They have been telling her "it's okay" instead of growling at her. They've been trying to understand the situation from her point of view. And they've been thanking her for doing her job.

If you tend to have a bad day at work *every* day, there may be a lesson in here for you. I'm JUST SAYIN'.

I Saw the Sign (and So Should Everybody).

There are many ways you can acknowledge inconvenience. Generally I am not a big fan of signs, but when you have something in your organization that is going to aggravate just about everyone, sometimes a humorous sign is the best way to go.

I fly out of Midway Airport in Chicago almost every week. There is one gate at Midway that my fellow frequent flyers and I look at as the "punishment gate." That's because the walk to it is very, very long. Like, longer than two city blocks long. (I know this because the hallway runs parallel with the street and I counted. I know, get a life, Liz!) But it doesn't end there. Not only is this hallway long and deserted (no stores, no food, no kiosks, no *nothing* until you reach the gate at the end), but some genius also decided that it might be fun to line this torturous hallway with thick carpet that makes you feel like you are dragging your suitcase through quicksand.

Well, there used to be a sign at the entrance to this distant gate that read:

Gate A4a, aka
Timbuktu, Never-Never Land, and
the Kingdom of Far, Far Away

Now, the sign didn't make the gate any closer, but at least it sent the message that the people running the airport understood what travelers were going through. That simple sign gave us all the perception that our efforts to walk through quicksand for two city blocks were not going unnoticed. And somehow, it made things better.

Rethink Your "Sorry."

Getting teams to acknowledge inconvenience is not easy. I believe that's because most people find the first step in acknowledging inconvenience—saying "I'm sorry"—to be so unpleasant. In fact, a lot of people actively resist apologies of any kind. I think there are two main reasons why.

First, some of us were told early in our careers that we shouldn't say that we are sorry. I remember receiving those very instructions in hospital orientation when I started my first job. The risk manager told us, "Don't ever say you are sorry because we can get sued." How nuts is that?!?

The other main reason why people don't like to say they are sorry is because we humans don't like to accept blame, especially when "it" is not technically our fault. That's why you will hear your team say things like, "Why should I say I am sorry? I am not the one who lost the lab tests," or, "It's not my fault Admitting never called us back."

Here's how to engage your team in acknowledging inconvenience. Tell them, "We say we are sorry in order to *express regret, not to accept blame.* What we're really saying is, 'I'm sorry you feel this way.' And when we do that, most people respond favorably."

Think back to the checkout example earlier in this chapter. As soon as the cashier said she was sorry, you recognized that the long wait wasn't her fault. The cashier expressed regret, and you did not blame her for the inconvenience.

Remember, to the patient or customer, your team is seamless. That patient doesn't really care whose fault "it" actually is, or what caused the current problem. All the patient wants is for us to acknowledge that the situation is lousy and to express regret.

I'd Like the Broasted Chicken, with a Side of Regret.

Here's one of my favorite stories about expressing regret. Every year, I used to go to Michigan with about 20 people who also worked in healthcare. So, you know, we were a nice, quiet, and subdued group. Ha! (And no, this had nothing to do with work. No conference or retreat—just a group of 10 friends from work and their spouses.)

One year, we went to a restaurant that didn't have a table big enough to seat all of us. We ended up outside on a porch. And since there wasn't a waitress or waiter assigned to the porch, the poor bartender was sent to take care of us.

When the food came out, everyone's meals arrived...except for the broasted chicken dinner my friend had ordered. Looking horrified, the bartender knelt down next to her and said, "I'm so sorry. The broaster is broken. Please tell me what else I can bring you; I'll put a rush on it! I'm really very, very sorry. I didn't know the broaster was broken when I took your order and I didn't find out until I picked everything up. I'm really sorry." (If you're not familiar with broasters, think of them as a combination between a pressure cooker and a fryer.)

"That's alright; just bring me a club sandwich," she replied.

Soon, the bartender returned with the sandwich, still full of apologies. "I'm sorry this happened. *So sorry* you had to wait."

My friend answered, "Hey, listen, it's okay. I know it's not your fault."

And then the bartender said something that stuck with me: "Well, it is my fault. I work for the restaurant."

WOW. After the bartender had walked away, my friend raised her eyebrows and said, "Hey, Ms. Liz, customer service queen, did you hear that?"

Yes, I did, and I was very impressed. This bartender-turned-porch-waiter had perfectly demonstrated the importance of expressing regret when acknowledging inconvenience. His apologies (which seemed to be sincere) totally changed my friend's perception of the situation. Instead of being angry that she had to wait longer than everyone else for her second-choice meal, she felt that the restaurant (or at least its representative) cared about her and was trying to please her. She was willing to brush the situation off with a "we're all human; no hard feelings" instead of getting upset and demanding to see the manager.

Here's the takeaway: As soon as that bartender acknowledged the customer's inconvenience and expressed regret for it, she "magically" turned into an understanding person. That's a trick we should all have up our sleeves!

But what if the bartender had come out and said, "We don't have your chicken. What else do you want?" My friend would have been ticked. She might have thought that the bartender didn't care about her and wasn't doing a good job. She definitely would have left with the impression that the restaurant didn't give two cents about its customers' experiences.

Just Say It!

It might not come easy for you or your team to say that you are sorry. I know that apologizing is not a common practice for many people! But if you think about how you would like to be treated (aka, which cashier's line you would choose), then it becomes clear.

Bottom line: We do things in the workplace that are awkward, embarrassing, and annoying—and most of us know it. Just as everyone working at the Midway Airport knows it stinks to have to go to that faraway gate, you know what rubs your customers the wrong way. But with just one sign recognizing the customers' inconvenience, their perception is that their efforts are not ignored.

When you get into the practice of acknowledging inconvenience, you'll see that this strategy works. You may even find yourself willing to admit that "sorry" is a small price to pay for happier customers. Not only will the amount of time and energy you put into service recovery be greatly reduced, you will also have a proactive approach to improving impressions and perceptions in your arsenal.

7

Service Recovery (Or, What to Do When "Oops" Won't Cut It)

Service recovery and acknowledging inconvenience. Aren't they really the same? Am I just splitting hairs by devoting a chapter to each? Well, yes and no. As I said in the previous chapter, acknowledging inconvenience is certainly a part of service recovery. Actually, it's the first step, and often, if you take that first step, you don't have to go any further.

If a simple, sincere expression of regret is going to fix a situation (think about the cashier and waiter examples in the previous chapter), then I call that "acknowledging inconvenience." But when the mix-up is bad, the gaffe is awful, or the blooper is a big one, and it takes more than a simple "I'm sorry," then, my friends, we have to move into full-on service recovery.

A "Real-Life" Example of Service Recovery

If you are married or have ever been in a long-term relationship, you know the difference between the things that a sincere "I'm so sorry, sweetie" will fix and those egregious errors that can be fixed only by a trip to the florist, a jeweler, or a five-star restaurant. Here's an example from my own life.

My husband, Frank, and I were married in October of 1981, and we were very poor that first year. I mean really, really broke. We bought a house the month before the wedding, and although it was the right decision, it made for tight finances—especially during the "newlywed" years.

February 1982 rolled around, and as I was doling out our meager budget, I put an extra $20 in both of our weekly allowances. "Valentine's Day is next week. Here's an extra $20 so that you can get me something for our first Valentine's Day!" I explained to Frank as I handed him the money.

I took my extra $20 and had fun finding some things for Frank. I bought a card and a blank cassette tape so that I could make a "mix tape." (HEY, it was the '80s!) I found Frank some cute Valentine's boxers and finished off the gift with some of his favorite candy. I couldn't wait for Valentine's Day.

When February 14th arrived, I brought out my gifts and gave them to Frank. He read the card, opened the gifts, and gave me a sweet kiss as he thanked me. Then I sat back and waited for my gifts. When none appeared, I asked Frank, "Where are my presents?"

He looked at me and said, "I'm sorry, but I forgot."

"Oh, okay," I responded. I was disappointed, but I knew that Frank had been working hard and in all likelihood he really *did* just forget. "It's all right, I understand. Just give me the $20 and I'll go shopping myself!" I wasn't mad, because I knew $20 could go pretty far at Kmart!

"I don't have it," Frank replied.

"What?!?" I screeched.

"I spent it," he admitted.

"How? On what?" I demanded.

"Well, you know last Friday I went out with the guys after work. Yeah, so Mark was a little low on cash, so I bought drinks for the both of us."

KABLOOIE! I went nuclear. Frank apologized a million times, but it wasn't enough for me. And back then, we didn't have the money for him to do any type of "service recovery."

In all fairness, and in the interest of total disclosure, Frank has been "recovering" from that first Valentine's Day for over 30 years. I always get the most beautiful flowers and the biggest cards, and he always takes me to my favorite restaurant for a lobster feast! The poor guy has more than made up for his first-year mistake, and it only makes me love him more.

What Is Service Recovery?

Service recovery is the art of moving beyond apologizing and actually *fixing* things that have gone wrong. It is especially important for leaders to understand the components of service recovery for two reasons. First, as the leader of a division, department, or shift, you will be running point when it comes to "fixing things." Second, you will need to demonstrate and teach service recovery methods to the people you work with so that you won't always have to be the one to "fix" everything.

Many organizations already have service recovery plans in place. They might range from filling out an incident report to empowering staff to use certain criteria to handle customer and patient complaints. But regardless of the form it takes, a good service recovery initiative should include three key components in addition to offering a sincere apology:

1. The person who discovers the trouble should be the one to fix it.
2. The patient or customer should be asked how he or she thinks the issue should be resolved.
3. Your staff should be trained in how to handle various types of incidents *before* they happen.

1: You saw it; you fix it.
First of all, the team member who hears the complaint, witnesses the problem, or discovers the trouble *has* to be the one to fix things. This is absolutely vital (and may seem obvious

to you), but I guarantee that you would be surprised by how many times this does *not* happen. Why? Most teams are more comfortable handing the problem off to their leader, or worse yet, a patient or customer service advocate.

What's wrong with advocates? Well, nothing! Let me state clearly that I have nothing against the fine people who work as advocates. It's just that the very best service recovery is always done as quickly as possible—preferably on the spot—and by the person who discovers the problem. When we send an issue to another department to resolve, the patient often gets the impression that we are not willing to address the issue ourselves. Plus, the patient has more time to fume and feel resentful!

One of the craziest things I have ever witnessed was a nurse calling the patient advocate from a patient's bedside. Yep, if I didn't see it, I might not believe it. I was observing this nurse's rounding, and one of her patients was upset because she had been promised that her lab results would be back in the morning—and it was already past 1 p.m.

I do believe the nurse was trying to be helpful. But in reality she was *really* off base when she said to the patient, "Let me call the patient advocate for you. I am sure they will be able to help." And with that she picked up the phone.

I don't think the patient thought much about it, but I was in the hallway practically jumping up and down. As soon as the nurse came out of the room, I took her aside and explained how she should have addressed the issue.

She should have said, "I am so sorry that your test results aren't back. Let me call the lab for you." Then the nurse should have picked up the phone right at the patient's bedside and contacted the lab, like so: "Hi, this is Sue. I am the nurse taking care of Ms. Smith today. She was assured her test results would be ready this morning and we still have not received them. Can you please check into this for me? I'll wait on the phone while you look…Oh great, they are ready, and you are going to put them in the system right now? Wonderful. Thanks for your help."

Now do you think Ms. Smith would be impressed? I certainly would!

I know from personal experience that fixing things on the spot has a huge impact on perception. About 15 years ago, I stayed at the Hyatt in Tampa while attending a conference. One day, instead of eating lunch with the group, I thought it would be nice to eat outside. (It was February and I live in Chicago, so the thought of eating outside was pretty appealing.) The hotel's restaurant was not open, but the bar, which served a light menu on the patio, was. Perfect!

The bartender was the only server. When he came to my table, I ordered an iced tea and crab cakes. (Hey, I just realized that this is my second bartender-turned-waiter story…maybe a theme?) Anyway, when this bartender brought the crab cakes to my table, he also brought silverware that was wrapped up in a napkin. After he walked away, I opened the napkin, only to find that the fork was caked with old, dried food. To make matters worse, there was not a spoon in the packet; just a knife.

Of course, I decided not to use that disgusting fork, and instead waited for the bartender to return. He was very busy and didn't come by my table for 10 or 15 more minutes. (In fact, he may have assumed that I was finished.) When the bartender *did* return, he seemed surprised that I hadn't touched my lunch. I showed him the fork, and he immediately understood. The first thing he did was apologize; then he brought me a clean one. Once again, all was right with my world. I ate my crab cakes, sipped my tea, and enjoyed being outside in February.

After I finished eating, I asked the bartender for the check. He told me there wouldn't be a bill, because of the mix-up with the fork. I was stunned! I hadn't even been that upset, and yet the bartender addressed the issue himself, on the spot, without hesitation. Some 15 years later, whenever I am in the Tampa area, I still stay at that hotel because its bartender waived a $20 bill for crab cakes and iced tea.

I think it's fair to assume that when we resolve a customer or patient issue ourselves, as soon as we become aware of it, those people will develop the same type of loyalty!

2: Ask, and you shall receive an answer.

The second step in service recovery is asking the patient or customer how you can best resolve the issue. You might be surprised to hear that most people—our 90 percenters—will ask for very little. (Often, that's because they don't know what to ask for! We have a plan to deal with those people, so stay tuned for Step 3.) But for now, back to Step 2…

When there is a problem and we ask the patient or family, "How can we fix this?" we win on two fronts. First, we put ourselves in a position to resolve the matter. And second, we have given the patient or family the perception that we regret the incident and are taking responsibility for making it better. We are not ignoring them or the issue.

Again, I know from experience (and I bet you do too) how good it feels to be asked, "How can we fix this?" Last year I traveled from Phoenix, Arizona, to Flagstaff, Arizona, via car. Because I was making the trip late at night and knew that the roads would be dark and curvy, I hired a sedan service (meaning that a professional driver would be taking me). The trip was supposed to take about two and a half hours, but I was going to be charged for five hours to cover the round trip. I was staying at the *Radisson* in Flagstaff. That tidbit is important, so remember it!

My driver seemed nice enough, but I thought she was a little cavalier when I asked her if she knew the directions. "Flagstaff is not that difficult to navigate; I'll figure it out when we get there," she told me.

That did not inspire much confidence, so I probed a bit more. "Don't you have a GPS?" I asked.

"Yes," she replied, "but I don't need it."

Okay, fine, I thought. Well, as you probably guessed, when we got into Flagstaff we were driving…and driving…and driving…in circles. At one point, I suggested it might be time to turn on that GPS.

"Relax," the driver snipped at me. "We are NOT lost."

Now I was ticked off. "I know that when I have been past the same building three times, we are LOST!" I retorted.

The driver kept driving as I sat in the backseat fuming. Finally, she put on her turn signal as we approached a hotel on the left. I read the sign and rolled my eyes. If I was a nicer person, I might have spoken up at that point. But I was aggravated, so I let the driver pull into the hotel's parking lot. When we rolled to a stop at its front door, the driver turned around and said to me, "I *told you* we weren't lost!"

"This is the *Ramada*," I replied with as much condescension as I could infuse into my voice. "I'm staying at the *Radisson*!"

When I finally got to the correct hotel, the first thing I did was call the sedan service that woman worked for. I was angry. I was *furious*! I wanted to give the driver's manager an earful. And the next day, I promised myself, I would tell my office *never* to book me with that company again!

When the manager came to the phone, I gave him a blow-by-blow of the situation, making sure he knew exactly how outraged and annoyed I was. What he did next was a great example of service recovery.

First, the manager apologized profusely, so much so that *I* began to feel sorry for *him*. What he *didn't* do was excuse the driver's actions or defend her conduct. Then he asked me, "Ms. Jazwiec, how can I make this right with you?"

After a few moments' thought, I realized that what was irritating me the most was that my bill for the sedan service included an automatic 20 percent gratuity. The last thing I wanted was for this driver to get a tip, so I said to the manager, "I don't think I should have to tip the woman."

"Done!" he answered without hesitation. "Anything else?" Again, I was surprised, but thought to myself, *Well, as long as he's asking…* I replied, "I did drive around in that car for over a half hour while the driver was lost."

"Okay," the manager replied, "how about this? We will credit your bill for the entire gratuity and two hours of travel time." Wow! I was impressed and delighted. And yes, I still use that transportation company when I am in the Phoenix area.

Now, some of you might be thinking, *Why didn't you ask for the whole trip to be comped?* Oh, I definitely thought about it. But when the manager was so very nice to me on the phone, I went from being a 10 percenter to a 90 percenter. I realized that the driver's bad service wasn't his fault; in fact, he never once defended her actions. He acknowledged my inconvenience and did everything in his power to make the situation right. Perhaps he would have comped the entire trip if I'd asked, but that isn't the point.

The point is, this service recovery was individualized to address my issues. And that's what made it so special.

3: Know it; don't wing it.

Step 3 in service recovery is having a program in place. Team members need to know ahead of time how to address issues when they arise. They also need to be familiar with the exact parameters and limits of the "fixing."

When Quint and I worked together at Holy Cross Hospital in Chicago, he put in a service recovery strategy that enabled anyone in the organization to use up to $250 to fix a service issue on the spot. It was especially used to fix the issues stemming from lost or missing personal belongings.

Now, this was quite a departure from our normal course of action. And at first, our team was very skeptical. "We're going to be robbed blind!" some colleagues worried. "We're in a tough neighborhood. When word on the street gets out, we're done for."

But guess what? That didn't happen, because you know why? We always ended up paying that money anyway—but after a lot more wasted time and trouble.

Do your patients regularly lose robes, phones, and glasses? I used to think there must be a magnet in the hospital that just pulls out people's dentures and hearing aids.

Before Quint arrived, our way of handling the inconvenience of losing a patient's belongings was to accuse the patients themselves. It was brutal. Does this situation sound familiar?

PATIENT: "Excuse me, nurse, I can't seem to find my jacket."

NURSE: "Really? You are just noticing that now after being in the hospital for three days? Are you sure you had one? Maybe your family members took it home."

PATIENT: "No, I already asked my family, and they don't have it."

NURSE: "Hmm, really! Are you *sure* you had one? You had some strong pain medicine last night; maybe you just dreamed you had a jacket."

PATIENT: "I KNOW I had a jacket!"

NURSE: "Okay, okay. Well, I am going to have to fill out a form, and someone will come and talk to you."

At this point you might think that the interrogation was over. But you'd be wrong. Next, the risk manager comes up and talks to the patient.

RISK MANAGER: "Now, I understand we have a jacket incident we need to discuss."

PATIENT: "Yes, I came in with a jacket and now it is missing."

RISK MANAGER: "Really? Are you sure you had it with you, or did your family take it home?"

PATIENT: "Yes, I'm sure, and no, my family did not take it home! I told that to the other person."

RISK MANAGER: "All right, no need to get testy, just doing my job. Let's say I believe your jacket is missing. How much did it cost?"

PATIENT: "It was $75."

RISK MANAGER: "Seventy-five dollars for a jacket! It must have been some jacket! Do you have evidence of that, and do you have the receipt?"

PATIENT: "Yeah, I always carry the receipt in my back pocket. What are you, crazy?!?"

By this time the poor patient is feeling like a thief instead of the wronged person. (In case you were wondering, being interrogated is even worse for perception than being ignored.) And guess what? Some three to four weeks later, after some more forms are filled out and more approvals are given—and after the incident has been moved from department to department—Finance is requested to send a check in the amount of $75 to the patient. And we wonder why that patient is not more appreciative of our efforts.

So, Quint got rid of that ridiculous procedure and replaced it with one that was much simpler and more customer friendly. Here's how the new conversation between patient and nurse went:

PATIENT: "You know, I had a jacket here when I came in and it's no longer in my room. I asked my family, and they don't have it."

NURSE: "I am very sorry that happened. May I ask you how much the jacket cost?"

PATIENT: "It was $75."

NURSE: "Thank you. I will take care of this."

The nurse would walk down to the security office where the service recovery fund was kept and sign out $75 for the patient. Then she would return to his room, hand him the money, and say, "We are very sorry that your jacket was lost."

Now people were convinced that we would go out of business doing this...But HELLO! When folks lose things, we end up paying them anyway. Right? Of course we do! AND this way, we eliminated at least four hours' worth of work for the rest of the organization, which saved us much more than $75.

We did not spend any more money than we normally did out of our service recovery program, but there was a huge difference in the patients' perception. Quint's strategy wasn't just about throwing some dollars at the problem. The money represented that we respected our patients' time and that we regretted their inconvenience. And hopefully, the entire strategy made each person feel valued.

Most important, we gave our patients the impression that we were concerned about their losses. The old way of dealing with lost items made our patients feel like criminals, while the new way made them feel special, noticed, and heard. It knocked their socks off! And once the staff got used to the new procedure, they agreed that it felt pretty good to be able to fix things. Not surprisingly, we began to notice a huge difference in our patients' perception.

Okay, now here's the point I've been working toward: If you don't have a service recovery program in place, positive changes in perception (like what happened at Holy Cross) never happen. Think about it this way: Things get screwed up and go wrong in day-to-day work life—you will never be able to change that. Surgeries get delayed, tests have to be repeated, items get lost, etc. I believe most of our patients and customers understand that. What they can't understand is us not fixing those issues, or not sending someone else in to address their problem.

Having a plan in place—and thereby nipping patient and customer dissatisfaction in the bud—is such an easy solution. Why *wouldn't* you do it?

Now, of course I understand that not all of you will be able to put a $250 program in place. Don't worry; there are other plans you can use. Start by thinking about the things that are the most likely to go wrong in your department, decide how to best handle them, and have a best practice ready to deploy. For instance, if you know your department can get backed up and run late for appointments, you might want to get gift cards to a coffee shop and accompany them with a little note that reads, "Sorry we were running latte!" (Okay, I'm sorry, but I love puns.)

Here are a few real-life examples: Once, I worked with a post-partum unit that kept "sleep kits" handy. The kits contained an eye mask, ear plugs, and some lavender linen spray. Nurses gave these kits to new moms who complained that they couldn't sleep well with all the activity on the unit. I also encountered a valet parking team that gave away gift certificates for car washes anytime someone had to wait more than 15 minutes to get their car. Are you getting the idea?

The Right Tools for the Right Results

I stay in hotel rooms all the time. And from time to time, things go wrong. Heating systems fail, outlets don't work, and heaven forbid, the remote control for the TV goes on the fritz. During one hotel stay, my room's air conditioning was broken. The only setting that would work was 60 degrees, so I had two options: freezing or shutting the unit off and steaming. Neither seemed attractive, so I called the front desk and asked them to send someone to fix the problem.

Soon, a man arrived at my door, and he fixed the problem quickly. I was happy, but then he handed me a little cellophane bag with a chocolate wrench, screwdriver, and hammer in it. Need I say more? Chocolate tools! How clever, how fun, how yummy!

Listen, we all know that we are going to have screwups! But that's why we have service recovery. When done well, it can have remarkable results. In fact, there are many studies that have found that people whose complaints were addressed during their service experience actually had better satisfaction than people who never experienced a problem at all!

When our service recovery plans include the three things I mention in this chapter (the person who hears the problem fixes the problem, the individual is asked how best to resolve the issue, and a program is in place to address the most common problems), we not only master the art of service recovery, but we leave our patients and customers with the perception that they are important and valuable to us.

8

WOW Vs. WHOA
(Or Should It Be "WOE"?)

Picture this: You walk into the institution. Someone takes down your information, and an identification wristband is placed on your arm. You are escorted to an assigned room, asked to get undressed, and given a standard-issue garment to put on. Your valuables are logged and may be placed with security for safe-keeping. You are told when your meals will be served, when you can leave the room, and when you need to have lights out for sleep.

Patient or Prisoner? Client or Crook? Classmate or Inmate?

Honestly, there are times when we all treat our customers, patients, and students like they are criminals. And yes, I understand that there are some really good reasons for doing things the way that we do. But remember, we are focusing on perception here. And the truth is, we do some things that we think are fine, but that are actually so far from "wow" that they end up in the "whoa," "woe," or "oh no" categories. Without intending to, we drive the customer crazy!

Most of the time, I don't think we realize the impact these things are having because they are policies or regulations that have been in place for a long time, or are habits that have just crept into our lives over the years. That's why, in this chapter, my goal is to help you start thinking about whether your organization's standard procedures make your patients or customers say "wow" or "whoa."

I Don't Care *Why*. I Care About How I *Feel*.

I used to shop at a well-known chain drugstore. When I first started going there, the razor blades were kept in a locked case. You know the type: You have to press a button and wait for someone to come with a key. It was a little inconvenient, but I tolerated it. I understood that those were expensive and dangerous items that could be easily pocketed.

Over time, this store started to put a few more items in those locked cases. It started to irritate me. It seemed I could never get everything on my list without having to wait at least twice for an employee to come and open up a case.

One day I went into the drugstore and I promise you, *everything* on my list was under lock and key. I went to get facial moisturizer: locked. Antacid pills: locked. Cold medicine: locked. Razors: locked. An in-home test kit: locked. I wanted to tell the dude with the keys, "Just walk around with me. I'm tired of pushing buttons and waiting for you."

The last thing I needed was some eye drops. When I went to the shelf, you guessed it: LOCKED. I pressed the button, and this time the store manager came. I told him how frustrating, irritating, and annoying all the locked cases were.

He turned to me and said, "Ma'am we have to do this. We have a lot of theft in this store."

That answer didn't help me at all, so I replied, "So your solution is to treat me, and all your paying customers, as THIEVES!"

That was my impression. Maybe not the correct one, but nevertheless, it was my perception that I was being treated like a common criminal. I have stopped shopping at that drugstore.

We have to be very careful of the impressions we create (perhaps unintentionally) that make our patients or customers say, "WHOA!" This will probably take some work on your part, because as I've said, we often don't realize the effect our words and actions are having. We do things that have become such a part of our common practice that we fail to realize the negative impact they might be having.

Remember my closing the curtain story? The one in which we started telling our Emergency Department patients that we were closing the curtains for their privacy and found out that previously many people over many years had gotten the impression that we were closing the curtain because we did not want to look at them? Yeah, those things are out there. Whether you want to believe it or not, they're in your organization, too!

Brainstorm Your Way to Better Perceptions.

I sometimes do an exercise with my audiences called "wow vs. woe." It's a tabletop exercise in which people brainstorm things that might wow the patient or customer and things they are currently doing that can bring the patient or customer grief. It's a very interesting exercise; I strongly suggest you do it sometime.

I have always loved the answers people come up with in the woe category. Some of my favorites are:

- Weighing patients at 5 a.m.
- Waking patients up to take a sleeping pill
- "Semi-private" rooms (Don't even get me started on them!)
- Patient gowns…of course
- Oh, and dead plants in the surgical waiting room. I mean, if you can't take care of a philodendron, what's going to happen to the guest's loved one? (I have to thank Dennis Snow, a wonderful speaker who specializes in the customer experience, for that one. Dennis has a Disney background, and he was taught there that "everything speaks to the guest.")

And my very favorite woe: wood chips in the toilet paper. WHAT?!? Yep, evidently someone purchased really cheap toilet paper, and you could actually see little chips of wood in it. Now, I am telling you, that does not exactly give *anyone* the right impression.

Whom Are You Treating?

The point of the "wow vs. woe" exercise is to get people to think about whom they are treating: themselves or the patient. Let me use myself as an example of what I mean.

I am a big woman. I know I could stand to lose a few pounds (okay, more than a few). Let's say that tomorrow I fall off of a stage and break my leg. It's a bad break and I need to have surgery in order to fix the bone with a pin. Now, I can pretty much bet that when I am admitted, some good doctor or dietician is going to put me on a 1,200-calorie diet while I am in the hospital.

But really, who is that helping? I am going to tell you that it's *not me*! Those two or three days I am in the hospital are not going to have a huge impact on my lifestyle. Again, yes, I recognize that I could lose some weight, but if I have to be in the hospital for three days with a broken leg, I want ICE CREAM!

Now is not the time to send me on a weight loss journey. Maybe once I am discharged and beginning rehab, I would be more open to talking about my lifestyle. But yeah, during that initial hospital stay, if you asked, "Liz, while you are here, would you like us to start you on a reduced-calorie diet?" my answer would be, "I understand, but I am stressed and scared and my LEG is BROKEN, so cottage cheese is just not going to cut it." (Oh, and by the way, having ice cream for three days isn't really going to hurt my healing.)

Orders like reduced-calorie diets are instituted because they are routine. I understand that. But sometimes our routines are crazy! They don't serve the patients; they serve us. Admit it: We have some crazy policies in our organizations. (And we all know the root of the word "policy" is "police.")

Frequent Elevator Flier

Quint came across a ridiculous "woe" policy early in his time as senior vice president at Holy Cross Hospital. At HCH we had several meeting rooms, including the boardroom on the top floor of the hospital. Quint's office was on the first floor, so he did a lot of elevator riding in order to attend meetings.

One day, Quint noticed there was a man in the elevators as much as he was. And over the next two days, almost every time Quint got into the elevator, this gentleman was also there. And he wasn't getting on or off at the first floor. Finally, Quint's curiosity got the better of him and he asked this man where he was going.

The man told Quint that, unfortunately, both of his parents were in the hospital: his mother on the 3rd floor, his father on the 6th. Quint asked the man, "Wouldn't it be easier if they were on the same floor, the same room even?" (Yes, we still had "semi-private" rooms.)

The man said, "Of course! I inquired about that, but was told it is against hospital policy."

Quint assured the man he would look into the matter. He thought that surely this man was mistaken, and that there must be another reason why his parents couldn't be closer together. Perhaps sharing a room would be a bit out of the ordinary, but the same floor should have been an easy fix.

WRONG! Quint found out that there was actually a written policy barring any two patients with the same last name from being admitted to the same unit. *Why?* you might ask. Because the staff was concerned that orders or medications might get mixed up. *Okay*, you might think, *that makes sense, but* only *for the staff*. It was dreadful for that couple to be separated and a nightmare for their son.

Ultimately, Quint was able to arrange for the couple to be moved into the same room, and as you can imagine, it caused the staff some discomfort. But the move made things so much better for that family, whose perceptions mattered most.

When we serve ourselves instead of the patient or family, we will most often be giving the wrong impression. Yes, making a change to better serve the customer can make your life feel harder in the short run. But remember, in the long run you'll be improving service *and* perception, which will make life better for everyone (you included).

Genius? If You Say So...

Healthcare doesn't have a monopoly on crazy policies. Have you ever been to an Apple store? Now don't get me wrong; I love my Apple products. I absolutely can't live without my iPhone. But Apple has some wacky ways of doing business!

First off, the staff are called "geniuses." (When my husband, Frank, saw that on their shirts, he decided to buy a shirt that read "Einstein" for his next day at work. Oh that Frank…he makes me laugh every day.)

Now, trying to get a "genius" to help you…oh wow, that is a process…literally. A friend of mine told me that she went to the Apple store with a broken phone. When she arrived at the store, she was happy to see that it wasn't too busy. She approached the first "genius" she saw and asked if he could help her with her damaged phone. The genius replied that he would be happy to help, but as she started to hand him the phone, he walked away. My friend followed the genius to a computer, where he told her, "You need to request an appointment online."

"What?" she questioned. "Can't you help me now?"

"Of course I can," he smiled. "Just fill out this online appointment request!" My friend looked at the genius like he was crazy, but she needed her phone fixed, and evidently going over to a computer in the store and requesting an appointment was the only way that was going to happen.

WHOA! That is definitely a woe. Probably seems okay to those geniuses at Apple, but to us customers, it is a wacky policy.

Leave Me Alone!

Sometimes even when we try to do right, try to make a great impression, and try to put the customer's best interests first, we can still fail if we don't include the patient in the decision.

When you fail to include the customer's preferences into your plan, you can be sure that some of your best-intended strategies will fail.

We had a big fail back at Holy Cross Hospital. One of our committees decided that it would be nice to drop in on patients who did not have friends or family members visiting them. *Oh, how wonderful,* the committee thought. All these lonely people would now have someone popping in on them to say hi, ask how they were doing, and maybe even bring them a magazine or gift.

The committee also was intent on tracking their results, so they laid out their "Happy Visitors" plan with measurement in mind. First, they implemented it on just one Med-Surg unit, but not before studying the unit's baseline patient satisfaction scores. The committee would even be able to track individual patients' satisfaction thanks to a blind marker program that could identify the survey without divulging confidential information.

Finally, the people who volunteered for the program were trained. The patients without friends or family were identified. Everyone was excited, and the "Happy Visitors" started their mission. The committee could hardly wait for the monthly scores to come in. They were convinced that the people they visited would have a much better experience than the average patient. They anticipated that those short but effective visits would make a positive difference.

The scores came back and—you guessed it!—they were WORSE than those of the average patient. Significantly, statistically worse! *How could that be?* the team wondered. *What could be wrong?*

So they regrouped, gathered their Happy Visitors, and did more training. The committee made more resources available: magazines, videos, flowers, and almost anything the visitors could think of to make the program work. The Happy Visitors set out again, very determined. This time they spent even more time arranging flowers, reading newspapers, watching TV, and chatting with their new "buddies."

The results came back again. EVEN WORSE. Come on! This was devastating to the team. They were shocked. Their dreams of cheering up the lonely patients were crushed. What happened?

And then one committee member had an epiphany: Perhaps… just possibly…people who didn't have any visitors…(wait for it) DIDN'T WANT THEM. Maybe those people were all alone in the hospital because they liked it that way. Having strangers pop in to visit them was most likely their worst nightmare.

Our little committee did a lot of planning, but they left out one thing that turned this "wow" project into a "woe." They never asked the patients what they preferred! Yes, they trained the team, they gathered and examined data, they pulled together resources, but at the end of the day, they failed to take the most important step. They did not include the people they were trying to serve.

Can You "Hair" Me?

Not understanding the people we serve and what their needs are is a common cause of woe. I used to go to a fancy schmancy hair salon. You know the type; almost all of us have visited one of those at some point or another. They draw you in with the elegant look of the place, the staff who have the weirdest hair in the world, and the impression that if you get your hair done there, *Vogue* magazine will be featuring you on their next cover.

At this particular salon, you had one person (a colorist) do your color and another person (a hair designer) do the cut. My colorist was a man named Robare, and my hair designer was named Chloe. Now, with my travel schedule, when I need my hair done, I NEED my hair done. So I called to make an appointment for the only day I was available that week. The receptionist (who always sounded bored or annoyed) told me that Chloe had only one opening at 1 p.m., but Robare was not open at 12. He had only a 2 p.m. opening. I said, "Fine, put me with Chloe at 1 p.m. and then Robare can do my color afterward at 2 p.m."

"That's impossible!" she screeched. "You must have your color done first!"

"I know that is the preferred way to do it, but I need to get my appointment done on that day, and it seems like a good solution to me," I replied.

"It cannot be done in that order," the receptionist insisted.

"Of course it can. I don't mind," I assured her.

"You can't make that decision!" she snapped.

"IT'S MY HAIR!" I retorted.

Now I would like to tell you that the receptionist saw the light and I got my appointment...but no, I did not. The fancy schmancy salon won. They couldn't change their policy. I, of course, found a new place to get my hair done—one where the rules weren't quite so strict!

As we try to improve perception in order to create better experiences for patients, families, and visitors, we have to include them in our plans. We have to ask them, "Would you like to start on a diet while you are here, or would you rather have ice cream?" Or, "We noticed there are not many people stopping by to visit. Would you like some company? There are volunteers who would be happy to pop in." Or, "We can work you in if you get your hair cut before the color."

Get it? I promise you, when we fail to include the people we serve in our decisions or plans (even if our intentions are good!), we are bound to come up with a lot more "whoas" or "woes" than "wows."

9

The WOW! Factor (Or, the Power of Getting Personal)

"Wow service," "wow perception," and "wow experience." Yep, we hear those phrases all the time, and for good reason. You have to wow your patients if you want high perception scores. If you wow your clients, they will become loyal. The key to customer satisfaction is the wow factor. And in the previous chapter, I mentioned how important it is to turn "whoas" and "woes" into "wows."

That seems so daunting, doesn't it? It's an easy word to say, but in practice, "wow" is a really big thing to accomplish. It's right up there with "thrill," "marvel," and "sensational." Those aren't everyday words; those are more like things that happen once a year. How are we supposed to do that in our busy, stressful, day-to-day work lives?

It's a challenge to try to come up with "extraordinary" on a regular basis. Heck, it was even hard for me to write this chapter. You know I love to tell stories, but even for me, it was difficult to come up with more than one or two amazing stories of being "wowed" as a customer—stories that seemed truly spectacular, you know, over the top.

So I asked my friends and family for "wow" stories. My sister, Donna, shared one with me that I thought was special.

"You Did the Right Thing!" (A Reassuring Email)

My niece Lauren was in Ireland doing a summer internship as part of her studies for her college degree. The family had also planned a big vacation to Australia and were planning to fly out on the day after Lauren returned from Ireland.

Well, as sometimes happens with all of us (or with our children), Lauren somehow didn't arrive at the airport in Ireland on time. It was too late to board, so she missed her flight. And now the *whole* family was at risk of not getting to Australia if Lauren was not back in the United States to fly with them.

My sister, Donna, was a frequent flyer with Continental (now United). So she called the airline, reached an agent named Kathy, and explained the problem. Kathy told Donna that there was one seat left on the next flight, but it was in first class and was very expensive. The alternative to booking that pricey flight, Kathy explained, was for Lauren to try to fly on standby, since there were no other seats available for any flights that day. On the previous flight just one or two passengers were boarded from standby, Kathy said. Since one of those seats was Lauren's, my sister didn't have much hope.

With no good options available, Donna mulled her choices over with Kathy, the agent. She really didn't want to have to pay so much for the flight, but with the standby option there was a chance that the entire family would *all* have to miss their flight to Australia. Knowing how much it would screw up their plans if Lauren didn't get on that next flight as a standby passenger, my sister bit the bullet and purchased the first class seat.

About an hour and a half later, my sister got an email from Continental. Donna didn't remember giving the agent her email address, meaning that Kathy must have looked it up in Donna's profile. The email said that the flight ended up being oversold in economy, and that Lauren would never have been pulled off standby. Kathy confirmed that Donna had made the right decision in purchasing Lauren the first-class seat. My sister had not asked the agent to follow up, but Kathy's message made her feel so much better about spending the extra money.

It's All About Getting Personal.

When Donna told me the story, she said, "It was a simple thing on the agent's part, but it had a huge impact. It made such a big difference to me."

And that, ladies and gentlemen, is the big secret to "wow" service. Read Donna's quote again: "It was a simple thing." In putting together this book, and this chapter in particular, I have come to the realization that "wow" service isn't thrilling, marvelous, or sensational. It is PERSONAL! And personal does not have to be made of big, showy stuff. It can be small acts, like a simple email. Personal can be as basic as a cup of ice (see Chapter 3). Personal is the grocery store clerk apologizing for the long lines.

In today's world, it seems as though many of us are treated as numbers instead of people. That's why personalized attention always leaves us with the best of impressions and leads to "wow" service. It's why we don't have to come up with extraordinary things every day in order to improve perception. That's good news if I've ever heard it!

All we need to do to "wow" our patients or customers is to make a personal connection. If you think that's impossible, it's not. But it will require you to adopt a different way of thinking. You'll have to think like the patient or the customer. In my sister's example, I am sure that agent was thinking, *Boy, if that were me, I would sure like to know that I had made the right choice.*

Organizations that do a great job of service have already figured this out: Personal is not necessarily extravagant. For example, at one hotel chain, the bellman looks at your luggage tag as he takes your bag out of the car. Then he uses his earpiece walkie-talkie to contact the front desk and tell the clerk your name. By the time you approach the desk, the host greets you with a "Welcome, Liz, we've been expecting you." For me that inspires a "wow" reaction, but in reality, it is just a very nice personal touch.

Now, if you don't mind, I'd like to share two more "wow" stories I've collected that really show the power of the personal touch.

A Crafty Conference

Mary, a friend of mine, told me that one of the best parent-teacher conferences she ever attended was with her son's fourth grade teacher. This came as a surprise to her, because she was actually kind of dreading the meeting. Her son Bill was a smart kid, but he could also be a handful. Sitting still and listening were not among his skill sets. Most of the parent-teacher conferences Mary had attended could be boiled down to the same message: Bill could be a very gifted student, *if* he buckled down and tried to learn.

So with a bit of apprehension, Mary and her husband walked into the classroom, expecting to be seated across from the teacher's desk as usual. But this night, when they walked in, the teacher asked them to join her at a round table in the back. "Please have a seat. I want to start this meeting off a little unconventionally," she said. "So if you will indulge me, let's begin with a craft project."

My friend looked at her husband just as he was rolling his eyes and jabbed him in the stomach.

The teacher continued, "I've done most of the work for you." When Mary and her husband looked on the table, they could see their son's name spelled out on a piece of paper that was hanging from a rainbow. "All I am asking the parents to do is help me come up with some adjectives that best describe their children," the teacher explained. "I will hang these rainbows tonight so that when the children come back in the morning, they will see them all around the classroom.

"I thought I would make it easy on you and use BILL instead of WILLIAM," she laughed, and then continued with the instructions. "I'd like to think of an adjective starting with each letter in Bill's name."

As the three of them talked about Bill's strengths, the words came easily: Bright, Inquisitive, Lively, and Loyal. When she told me this story, Mary commented that it was so nice to start the conference with her son's strengths instead of his weaknesses. She also told me that having Bill's teacher share in the task of identifying his most endearing traits also meant that she really knew and understood Bill.

Of course, Mary, her husband, and the teacher *did* eventually get around to, "Liz would do so much better if she just applied herself." OOPS, did I say "Liz"? Yeah, you can bet my parents heard that line year after year, as well…

My point is, writing adjectives on strips of paper is not spectacular. But for Mary, her husband, and Bill, it was unexpected, refreshing, and personal. It was a wow.

Yes, I Know You'd Like Some Creamer with That.

In Chapter 8, I told a story about a whoa/woe experience I had at a fancy schmancy hair salon. (They refused to cut my hair before they colored it, remember?) Now, I'd like to balance that out by telling you a story about Mario, the best hair designer and makeup artist in the world!

If you ever wonder why I never look like my pictures, it's Mario's fault. He does my hair and makeup for any publication photos, and I always come out looking so much better than I do in real life.

I have been going to Mario for years. By now he knows me very well and treats me like a queen. But honestly, even early in my first few appointments with Mario, he always seemed to know what I like: French vanilla creamer in the coffee, cold water when I am shampooed, and a gossipy magazine while I sit with the color on my head. He knows to ask about my mother, he queries me about my travels, and he always finds one thing to compliment me about.

Years after I had been going to him, I asked Mario how he remembers all of that. I mean, now it is easy, but how did he do it in the beginning? He said, "It's simple, Liz. When I first do someone's color, I have to make out a card with the formula so I'll be able to replicate it in the future. While I am doing that, I jot down some other things, such as, 'travels for a living, takes care of her mother, likes cold shampoos and French vanilla creamers x2.' The other stuff I just figured out," he laughed.

See, I knew that Mario did a great job on my hair on the first visit. But I knew I LOVED going to Mario on the second visit when he made it all about ME! So personal.

Do (or Give!) Them a Favor.

As I've (hopefully!) demonstrated, "wow" service is often individualized, but it doesn't necessarily have to be. Sometimes you can "do" personal on a grand scale. *What?* If you're thinking I am trying to confuse you, I am not. As always, I can best explain what I mean by telling a story. Here is a favorite of mine about a very creative director of Food and Nutrition Services.

I was assisting a hospital in Missouri with their service initiative. They had a "wow" service committee, and at one meeting, the director of Food and Nutrition Services gave a report on his department's "wow" initiative. They had teamed up with children's groups in the community—Girl Scouts, Boy Scouts, church groups, etc.—and asked them to make tray favors for the patients. If you don't know what a tray favor is, it is a simple little homemade item placed on a patient's food tray. It can be a card, or a little craft item such as a snowman made out of cotton balls or a butterfly made of pipe cleaners.

The program had remarkable success. At first only a couple of clubs made the favors, but as word spread and more and more patients and their families saw the favors, more groups wanted to get in on the fun. Schools and daycare programs joined in, local ladies' groups started making the tray favors, and even some teen clubs jumped on board.

Even though this was a hospital-wide initiative and every patient received the favors, it still included a deeply personal touch. It was personal to each patient because they knew the favor was not a store-bought product, that in fact, "Someone actually handmade this item for me."

The Card Says It All!

Personal can become customary, and that is pretty "wow" in itself. Here's another story about a standard practice one hospital put in place. This practice is one of my favorites because it's simple and brilliant.

Upon admission to the hospital, a greeting card is placed on each patient's chart—just clipped or attached to the clipboard, binder, or whatever. Everyone who touches the chart signs the card with their name and title. Joe from PT, Sue from Food and Nutrition, Patti the night nurse—they all sign their names.

The message inside the card is basically a "thank you." I believe it read something like, "It was our pleasure to care for you during your hospital stay." (There is probably more, but I have forgotten—you can fill in the rest.) When the patient is ready to go home, someone from the unit will walk in with the card and give it to the patient—often while the patient's family is also present. WOW! I can just imagine how some of those cards made the patient's day. I know some of them ended up on refrigerators or nightstands at home.

So individualized, so personal, so standardized, and SO EASY. Think about it: If you had to run around and get all those signatures when you were also getting the patient ready for discharge, this initiative would never succeed. But because it was a standard practice to put that card on the chart upon admission, it became an easy routine for the team and a wonderful surprise for the patient.

It is so surprising that when we think about what "wowed" us, so often it's not the big or great things; it's the simple little things: the sweet gestures, the thoughtful acts, or the kind words.

It's the Little Things.

We experienced many acts of kindness when my mother was in the hospital because of her aneurysm. I've already shared the "cup of ice" story, and here is something else that truly wowed me.

A couple of days after Mom's brain surgery, Debbie, her night nurse, said to me, "If the doctor okays it, I am going to wash your mom's hair tonight."

I said, "Thanks. That would be nice," but I really didn't think it was a big deal. I mean, my poor mom looked so awful—tubes and drains all over the place, the ventilator taped across her face, half of her hair shaved for the surgery. I just couldn't imagine that having her hair washed was going to make that much of a difference.

I came in the next morning, long after the night shift had left, and walked into my mother's room. As I approached the head of the bed, I saw my mom with her fixed-up hair. It was amazing! Debbie had not only washed my mom's hair, but because half her hair was missing, Debbie gave Mom a comb-over. (You know, kind of like Donald Trump or a '70s sportscaster!) Then I looked toward the corner of the room, and there was a large bottle of Suave hair conditioner. (Now, if you are in Infection Control, you'll just have to not read these next few lines.)

I was just about knocked over when I saw that bottle of conditioner. Here's why: First of all, in hospitals, large bottles like that are not allowed due to the risk of passing infections. So I knew that Debbie, or *somebody* in that ICU, had brought that conditioner in from home. Also, these days it is a big deal just to get your hair washed in the hospital because everyone is so busy. To get it washed, conditioned, *and* styled is a huge deal! I mean, just ginormous. I was blown away and deeply touched.

I looked back down at my mom in her bed. All the tubes were still there, and she was still not awake, but I felt better. I know it might seem silly, because under the circumstances hair care was such a small thing. The fact that my mother was on a ventilator in a coma for six weeks, without a single complication, is a testimony to the great care of her team of professionals. As a nurse, I understand that. But as a daughter, it was that bottle of Suave hair conditioner that made it easier for me to leave Mom every night, knowing that Debbie and the night shift team were caring for her exactly as I would.

A Familiar Face in an Unfamiliar Place

And how's this for an example of a tiny gesture that makes a huge impression? While I've never stayed there myself, I'm told there is a hotel in California that puts a very special memento in each guest's room. During the reservation process, you are asked if you want to upload a photo of someone you might miss: your kids, your spouse, or your dog, for instance. If you do choose to upload a photo, the hotel prints it, puts it in a pretty frame, and places it on your nightstand. Ta-da! When you walk into your room, you are greeted with a smiling face from home.

Is this a "wow" experience? Of course. Difficult? No. Personal? You bet. While a picture in a frame might seem like a very small thing, it's amazing how meaningful it is to glance over and see a photo of your loved one.

"Wow" is simply about doing things that touch people on an individual level. It doesn't have to be great big extravagant things. An email telling a mom she made the right decision, a warm welcome from a desk clerk, a little flag on your food tray on the Fourth of July, or a greeting card signed just for you—these things can make the biggest impact on a patient's or customer's perception.

There is one common theme in the stories in this chapter (and really, in this book): The things we do that create the biggest impressions and the very best perceptions are usually very simple but deeply personal.

10

Spin Your Wins: Tell 'Em What You're Doing Right

All right! You have gotten rid of your woes, personalized your wows, improved people's perception with words and actions, and created great impressions by managing expectations. Now what?

Spin it, baby!

What does that mean—spin? Well, in a nutshell, it means to tell people what you've done, share the good, and make the good do more. The definitions in the dictionary include "relate," "create," "prolong," and "extend."

The definition that I think best fits our application is "to present an interpretation (of a statement or event, for example), especially in a way that is meant to improve opinion." *Ohhh*, now that sounds political, doesn't it? That sounds wicked, right?

We would never do that with our patients or customers…but why not?

Okay, first, let me put out the disclaimer that I am not suggesting we make stuff up or create any falsehoods. We can leave that to the politicians and TV spokespeople. What I am suggesting here is that we simply do a better job of letting people know about all the good that we do.

Yes, You Have Permission to Brag.

We are so reluctant to tell the people we serve about our wins and our wows! Why are we like that?!? I think there are probably a couple of reasons; the first being that we are just not comfortable with sharing our accomplishments. Also, there are a lot of people in healthcare (as well as in other professions such as education and social services) who think it is wrong to "brag."

And then, there are other people, not quite as meek as the "anti-braggers," who think they shouldn't *have* to tell people about what's good in their organizations. The patients or visitors should have to figure it out themselves! Remember my curtain story? "Why should we have to tell these people the reason we are pulling the curtains?" Some of my team members thought the patients and visitors ought to just "get" it. They thought, *I am working hard enough as it is; now I have to tell these people all that I am doing for them, too?!?*

In a word, YES. Yes, you do need to tell these people all that you are doing for them. Why not? As I said before, it doesn't take any extra time, but it can make a big difference in perception.

For those of you who fall into the first category of "not wanting to brag," I have a bit of loving advice for you: GET OVER IT! If we are truly going to change people's perceptions, we have to get used to "bragging" or "spinning" or whatever else you want to call it.

Tell Them How Fantastic You Are.

Organizations that are known for their great customer service have one thing in common: They all tell you how fantastic they are. They all let you know that you are going to have a fabulous experience; in fact, some of them start telling you how great they are before you even engage with them!

As you know, I stay in hotels all the time. I've noticed that the ones that do a great job with service start telling you how wonderful they are on their websites as you make your reservation. There might be an award badge posted in the corner of the page, or a testimonial under a picture, and you might read a slogan like "Designed with you in mind." Yep, these hotels have "personal" already figured out.

When you get to the hotel, you might see awards posted in the front desk area, or a sign proclaiming "Best in Service" with a bunch of years listed. Little sayings such as "We do it best" or "Unique experience" might be printed on your key card holder. As you walk to the elevator, you'll probably pass a bunch of pictures on the wall showcasing the hotel's employees of the month.

Get it? Before guests have even gotten to their rooms, they've been given the impression that this is a hotel that does a great job with service. Why don't we do that? We do great work in healthcare, so why do we feel that we have to keep it a secret? TELL PEOPLE!

A Tale of Three Blankets

Here's my first example of how we can become better at "spinning." It is the tale of three blankets. Well, more than three blankets, really—it's about three healthcare organizations and their blanket stories.

First, let's start with a small rural hospital in Iowa. It has a big beautiful basket in its visitors' lounge. I saw the basket when I was touring with the CEO at the time, my buddy Greg Paris. We walked past the lounge, and the basket caught my eye because it was really a pretty big basket, maybe hand-crafted— just gorgeous. "What is that?" I asked Greg.

He turned and looked and nonchalantly replied, "Oh, those are blankets. We put them out at night. They haven't been picked up yet."

"Blankets?" Now I was curious, so I had to walk in and take a closer look at the basket. "They are!" I exclaimed. I was impressed. I mean, the basket was lovely enough on its own, but to be filled with blankets, well, how cozy was that?!?

"Do people know about this?" I asked Greg.

He said, "I think so, Liz, they are right here," and looked at me like I was daft.

"No, I mean, does everybody who comes to this hospital know that you put out a beautiful basket of blankets for visitors to have when they spend the night?" I asked.

Now it was Greg's turn to pause. "Well, no, we don't tell everyone; it's just something we do."

Do you see the missed opportunity to make a great impression? Imagine that your loved one is in the hospital, and in reading the admission handbook, under the visitors' section you see, "We are happy to provide blankets in our visitors' lounge to anyone who is here overnight."

You get it, don't you? Providing the blankets is wonderful, and you make an impression with the people who use them. But telling everyone about the blankets changes the perception of patients and families even if they never spend the night.

Okay, let's move on to blanket story number two. I was assisting a busy Emergency Department with their service initiative. While making rounds, I noticed that often, a nurse would bring a warm blanket to a patient. The patients seemed to really appreciate the blanket, and I thought it was a really nice touch. I asked the manager about the blankets, and she told me that the ED had two big blanket warmers, and that if patients would like a blanket, they could get one.

"How do they know?" I asked.

"Know what?" the manager replied.

"Know about the warm blankets. Who tells them?"

"Nobody tells them, but if anyone on the staff—nurses, doctors, techs, whoever—thinks that someone can use a blanket, they bring it," she answered me.

Okay, now that you've already read blanket story number one, you know what my next bit of advice was: YOU NEED TO TELL PEOPLE! I suggested that the ED make a sign for every patient room that read something like this: "Because we care and are concerned for your comfort, we have warm blankets available. We will be happy to bring you one. Just ask any of us!"

Get the spin? Here it is: The warm blankets are great, but if people don't know about them or need them, you get zero credit. However, when someone reads that sign—even if they don't want a warm blanket—their perception is that you care about them and that you are concerned for their comfort.

Okay, now for blanket story number three. My husband had surgery at a hospital in our area. It was not one that I was familiar with, though, so I didn't have my "Liz clout." Didn't matter; it was a very good hospital, and Frank received great care.

Frank was scheduled as the first case (Hey, I am no dummy. I know first is best.), so we were there very early, around 5 a.m. Frank was taken into the OR around 7 a.m., and I went into the family surgery waiting room. It was a large, lovely room with some couches and recliners, separated areas for TV watching or working, and, to my delight, coffee and donuts. I was very happy.

I got a cup of coffee and a donut and searched for my special spot. As I was looking around the room, I noticed that a lot of the people there had blankets. The volunteer wasn't in yet, so I asked someone who had a blanket where she found it.

"Oh, there is a big cabinet of them just under the TV," she directed me. And sure enough, when I opened up the two doors to this very large cabinet, it was chock-full of blankets. There must have been over 100 in there. Boy, was I happy: a hot cup of coffee, a fresh donut, and a blanket! I was all set to wait in comfort.

The issue is (and surely by blanket story number three you know what I'm about to say), this hospital didn't spin it. They didn't tell us about the blankets; we visitors had to find out about them on our own.

Think about this. You are a visitor waiting in Pre-op with your loved one, and someone hands you a card. It reads: We know this can be a long day for you as you wait for your family

member or friend. We are concerned for your comfort, so you
will find the following in our surgical waiting area:

- Hot coffee, tea, and chocolate
- Water
- Vending machines
- Sofas, recliners, and work tables
- Blankets (in the cabinet under the TV)
- Wi-Fi

All right, you get it. Now tell me something like that would not
make an impact. Of course it would! Again, even if you didn't
use the recliner or the Wi-Fi, the hospital still gets credit for
providing those things because it has taken all the nice things it
does for visitors and given them a good spin.

Show and Tell Others About Your Wins.

This is not just about blankets. (I know how literal some of us
get!) There are *many* great things happening in your organization. Every time something impressive is implemented, your
next thought needs to be, *How can we spin this?*

Let me help you get started. Put your awards and plaques in the
lobby, near the information desk or the seating area just inside
the door, so that they're one of the first things people see when
they enter the building. Let's face it; those awards help very few
people if they are stuck in the boardroom or CEO's office.

Here is a brilliant spin technique Quint taught us at Holy
Cross Hospital. When we brought in focus groups to discuss

the hospital's performance, we would ask the patients or visitors what they liked best. You might be surprised to hear that everyone shared something that they liked; yes, even the people who complained throughout the focus group meeting would think of something positive they had experienced.

Next, we would take each individual's picture and ask for a signed authorization allowing us to post the picture alongside the nice quote. When we displayed a photo, we added the neighborhood in which the person lived. So the caption might read, "'Everyone treated us like family!' —Mary Smith from Chicago Lawn." Quint knew that adding the neighborhoods would make things even more personal and spread the perception of the wide area we serviced. Yep, I told you it was brilliant.

Well, what if you updated that practice from hanging pictures on a hallway wall to posting them on your website? Imagine testimonials like that gracing your homepage. You could even post videos instead of still photos. Think of what a great first impression that could make! And best of all, this isn't a difficult strategy to implement; it just takes creativity and commitment to harvest those great remarks.

Here's another way to show and tell others about your wins: Feature them month by month! What I mean is, lots of hospitals, pharmacies, banks, schools, financial planners, etc. put out calendars every year. Yeah, I am talking about the old-fashioned paper kind. (Hey, people still like them!) To pick one example from that list, hospitals often use pictures of buildings or departments for the monthly photo. Boring! I mean, who wants to see a picture of an open MRI every day for a month?

So how about this instead? Many organizations pick an employee of the month; why not feature them in the calendar? Right? It's a double spin! It's great recognition for the team member, and you are also letting everyone know that you have compassionate, kind, caring individuals working within your organization.

Other Industries Use Spin Too.

Healthcare is one of the last industries to come around to "spinning wins." Other organizations have been doing it for years. Here's the thing: When done correctly, you don't recognize spin for what it is. That's why, although I have gotten very good at telling folks what they *should* spin, it's hard (even for me!) to always recognize when I've been spun.

Here is one "spin" I do recognize: Southwest and the other airlines never miss an opportunity to let you know when a flight has landed ahead of time. You might have heard it too: "Ladies and gentlemen, welcome to Chicago where the local time is 5:15, 10 minutes ahead of our scheduled arrival time of 5:25. Please keep that in mind the next time we are running a few minutes behind." This announcement usually elicits a little chuckle from the passengers, but make no mistake, it is a spin. And you can bet that the flight attendants have been instructed to share this type of win whenever possible!

Back to Blankets

I began my speaking career in 1997, and that's when I became an official road warrior. And back then, one of the most difficult things about traveling was trying to get a good night's sleep. If you think back to that time, hotel beds were awful! Bad polyester bedspreads that never seemed to be totally clean, pillows that were skimpy and were limited to one per person… and the *blanket*! That was the worst. It was either beige or green and made out of foam!

Getting a good night's sleep on the road was almost impossible. And then something wonderful happened: Westin introduced the "Heavenly Bed." And let me tell you, they knew how to spin it.

There was the usual marketing campaign, of course, but the best spin happened at the hotel. Like many things, I will never forget my "first time."

I was speaking in South Bend, Indiana, and had to go to Detroit. It's about a 200-mile trip without a lot of flight options, so I drove. And it was an awful drive. It was winter, it was snowing, and for the first part of the trip, I was in a near "white-out." Once I got to Detroit, it was dark and late, and I was lost. (This was pre-GPS.) When I finally reached my hotel, the Westin in Southfield, I was exhausted and *so much* in need of a good night's sleep.

Upon entering the hotel, I saw big banners showing people hugging pillows and blankets. The banners declared, "You are now in heaven!" Heaven? I thought I was in Detroit, but those people in the pictures looked so peaceful and so cozy that I allowed myself to hope.

I thought to myself, *Could this be true? Did I just stumble upon one of the hotels with the new beds, beds that are actually comfortable?*

As I approached the desk, I saw another banner across the back wall. It read, "The Heavenly Bed offers 10 layers of heaven starting with a pillow-top mattress." *WOW*, I thought to myself. *Maybe I am hallucinating.* After all, it was a four-hour drive and I was pretty tired.

Once my room was assigned, I received my key, and on the key holder I saw more encouraging news: "Here are the keys to a bit of heaven, right here on earth. Soothing weary travelers with an oasis of comfort and style, The Westin Heavenly Bed."

I was so excited to see this bed, I believe I was actually trembling in the elevator. As I walked down the hall to my room, I noticed that the privacy signs hanging on doorknobs had the same pictures of people sleeping in beautiful white beds. "I'm in heaven; please do not disturb."

I slid my key into my room's door, opened it up, and there it was! I could swear I heard trumpets blaring and angels singing. This beautiful white vision, so bright that the room felt illuminated just by its presence. White pillows—A LOT OF THEM. White comforter—NO FOAM. A mattress that wasn't only six inches deep. I couldn't wait another minute. I jumped on that bed and sunk into its wonder. Oh, yes, I was in HEAVEN!

I would have loved that bed no matter how the hotel promoted it. But it was their spin that gave me a truly great experience. The hotel's letting me know how much I was going to love that bed before I ever stepped a foot in the room took the experience from being great to being SPECTACULAR.

Start thinking about how you can tell and/or show your patients, visitors, and customers that you do a great job of service. You can start improving perception the minute people walk through your door, open your website, or check their calendars. It is not impossible; it is actually easy once you keep "spinning" at the front of your mind.

Quint was right when he taught us how to maximize our wins at Holy Cross. We *must* stop hiding our great work. When we share all the good things we are doing with the people we serve, it is not bragging; in many cases, we end up reducing people's anxieties. We change their impressions and make them feel at ease because they know we are going to do a great job.

In fact, if you don't implement anything else in this book, please put this tactic into practice. I am guessing that if we just gave our work a good "spin" and shared all of the outstanding things we do every day with our patients, visitors, and customers, we could make a huge impact on their perception.

Conclusion
See? It Really IS as Easy as PIE! (and Way Better Than Popcorn and Turkey!)

So that's it. Improving service excellence is about improving perceptions, and improved perceptions come from connecting with the people we serve. Plain, simple, beautiful, and extraordinary.

How did I—how did *we*—make it so difficult? Why do we resist connecting with our patients, students, and customers? How could so many of us have been blind to the reality that *connection* makes everything right in our work? It is exactly that connection that helps us make a difference and restores our enthusiasm and joy in what we do.

Service: The Ultimate Satisfaction Booster

Right now some of you might be thinking, *C'mon, Liz, joy?* Okay, maybe not dance-in-the-street, heart-bursting-with-happiness joy. But how about engagement? In Rich Bluni's book *Oh No...Not More of That Fluffy Stuff!*, one of the definitions Rich gives for engagement is "the opposite of burnout." So how about that? If not out and out joy, how about the opposite of burnout? Connecting with the people we serve can give us that. And that's why service is so important to me: because I have witnessed firsthand that when we connect with the people we serve, our morale improves!

Yes, I know there are a lot of other reasons why we focus on improving service. For many of us, it's in our organization's mission, and we all know it's the right thing to do. In healthcare, some of our payments are linked to patient satisfaction results. And as I have learned the hard way, if it's important to the CEO, you'd best get your behind on board.

But I believe the most compelling reason to focus on service is because *it makes the job better for us*. And if you are a leader, service makes the work better not just for you, but for your whole team.

I want to go back to shouting it from the rooftops. SERVICE MAKES WORK SO MUCH BETTER!

Trust me. Long-term satisfaction with our work is not about having a benefit plan or receiving a special bonus. Long-term satisfaction comes from knowing how we make a difference, and that the work we do has purpose and meaning. When we connect with the people we serve, our purpose becomes apparent. We *know* we are making a difference. I said this in my first book, in the first chapter, and it is only fitting that I say it again in this last chapter of this book.

What *Doesn't* Improve Employee Satisfaction

So many organizations try to improve employee satisfaction by giving out gifts at holidays (like turkeys for Thanksgiving) or by instituting random employee appreciation programs (like free popcorn day). And many organizations host award banquets for individuals with 10, 20, 30, or more years of service. Those rarely work. You know why? Because it just creates an entitlement mentality for the low performers. Think about it. You know some of those people being recognized with a service award are the worst people in the organization: Oscar the Grouch from Lab or Negative Nelly from Admitting.

Likewise, free popcorn never made anyone feel better about their job, and you can bet there were some people complaining about it. (It's too salty! You call this butter? The popcorn they gave us last year was soooo much better.)

And turkeys! Don't even get me started. One year at Holy Cross the organization gave out turkeys for Thanksgiving, and as a member of the administrative team, I shared the duties of passing out the turkeys. MAN! It was a nightmare. People complained that they didn't eat turkey, and some people wanted a gift certificate instead. One nurse asked if we could store hers in the freezer until Christmas because she didn't have enough room in her refrigerator. ARE YOU KIDDING ME?!? I wanted to say, "Take this flippin' turkey and give it to a neighbor, your mother-in-law, or a homeless shelter if you can't find room for it at your house!" (You know how I abhor people complaining about free food.)

No, those tactics really don't help improve employee satisfaction, because your low performers and complainers will always sabotage your best intentions.

However, when we immerse ourselves and our teams in purposeful, meaningful work, your good team members will be satisfied. And those are the types of people you want around you. Those are the people who will create a great culture: the individuals who light up when they know they have made a difference.

Getting Back to the Right Reasons

The truth is, making a difference is really what perception and personal attention are all about. And not so coincidentally, making a difference is why most of us choose our careers. People go into social work, education, and healthcare because we want to make a difference. We want to make things better for people. No one goes into our professions thinking, *Hmm, I would like a job where I could really aggravate people. What should I do…get a job with the DMV? Perhaps work for the IRS? Wait, I know! I will become a nurse—an ED nurse—then I can aggravate people who are sick. Jackpot!!!*

No one thinks that. We all go into our professions for the right reasons. Then somewhere along the way we get lost, start focusing on the wrong things, and become more negative with each year. That is certainly what happened to me, up until I was forced into a service initiative. An initiative that I vehemently opposed, by the way, but one that ended up bringing me right back to all the reasons I ever wanted to become a nurse.

I became a nurse because I wanted to reduce my patients' anxiety and ease their suffering. I wanted to make a difference. I wanted to make people feel better. When I was pressed into improving patient satisfaction, I didn't realize it at the time, but I was connecting back to all the things that are right about nursing.

This doesn't apply to just me. I have seen it happen over and over again. Organizations that do a great job at providing service excellence see an amazing improvement in employee morale and staff engagement. And here is why: It brings us back to our heritage, to the right reasons to do our work.

Not only do we choose our professions because we want to make a difference; it is why our professions were created. Social work was created to improve people's circumstances, and we know that education makes a colossal difference in people's lives.

But try as I might to be inclusive of everyone's occupations, I can speak personally about only my industry. Healthcare was begun to make people feel better, to make them more comfortable, to make a difference. No other profession should be better at delivering service with care and compassion than us. That is our birthright! And when those of us in the healthcare field connect to that birthright, pride and joy return to our work.

The Simple Things Make the Biggest Difference.

There are a lot of stories in this book that really demonstrate how the simplest things can make a difference. A bottle of conditioner, a warm blanket, a friendly welcome. And, of course, we know that it is not really the blanket or the conditioner that has the biggest impact; it is the personal connection it makes, the feelings and the perception it conveys. The welcome that makes you feel at home, the blanket that lets you know somebody cares, the little touches that can leave a lifelong impression.

Let me finish this book with one of my all-time favorite stories about how changing a perception can create an excellent experience.

I was assisting a hospital in Texas, and in a meeting the CEO said, "Liz, I want to tell you a story about scripting. We have a patient—his name is Henry—and he has been very sick over the last two years. He has been admitted 12 times.

"Every time Henry is with us, at some point during the stay, I come down to my office and find his wife sitting on my sofa, waiting to meet with me. She always has a list of things that we are doing wrong."

So the CEO wasn't surprised the previous week when, on Henry's 12th visit, his wife was once again waiting on his sofa. "How's Henry?" the CEO asked.

She replied, "He's doing okay, about as well as we can hope for." The CEO waited for the list of complaints.

Henry's wife began, "I must tell you something…" The CEO waited for it. "…Something is different on this visit, something has changed…" He braced for it. "Almost everyone who has come into Henry's room has asked him, 'Is there anything else I can do for you? Is there anything else you need? Anything we can get for you?' Sometimes they even asked ME!"

The CEO smiled because he knew this was a campaign that the hospital had been working on. "I'm very happy to hear that."

Henry's wife went on to say, "Do you know this was the first time since Henry has gotten sick that I actually felt comfortable enough to leave the hospital? I knew that if he needed anything in the middle of the night or if there was anything he wanted, that there would be someone there to help him. I actually went home and slept in my own bed."

WOW…that's a big deal…isn't it? It's huge. If you've ever had a loved one in the hospital, you know it is not easy to spend the night at the bedside. Even if the staff bring you a recliner or a cot, it's just not comfortable. Henry's wife had done this over 30 times in the past two years. Being able to go home at night, sleep in her own bed, and take a shower like a human being was a big, big deal. It totally changed her experience.

The reason this story still gives me goose bumps, still touches me, is because I knew the team at this hospital. They were *always* willing and able to take care of Henry in the middle of the night. They didn't make any operational changes, they didn't change the way they were working, and they didn't change any results or outcomes. There were no major quality improvements. The only thing that changed on visit 12 was the *wife's perception of care* because people asked, "Is there anything else that I can do for you?"

Please don't ever think that service or perception is frivolous, or that creating great impressions doesn't matter all that much. To Henry and his wife, it made all the difference in the world. And more importantly, it made a tremendous difference to that team. They began to feel better about their work. Once they understood how a simple question could change the patient's experience, they embraced it. Once they connected improved perceptions with service excellence, they were proud of the difference they were able to make for patients and families.

All of you deserve to feel great about the work that you do. I have been very blessed these past several years because I've been able to spend time with people in all kinds of positions in all sorts of industries. And although we have our differences, there is so much that we share. It tickles me when I speak to folks outside of healthcare and they laugh at my ED stories. I am lifted when people share with me that when they do better for others, they feel better about their work. And I am deeply humbled whenever those feelings can be attributed to something I may have written or said.

It has been a privilege to share these thoughts with you in this little trilogy of mine. I am deeply grateful for all of your kind words and support.

Love,

Liz

Resources

Access additional resources at www.studergroup.com.

ABOUT STUDER GROUP:

Studer Group® helps bring structure and focus to organizations through the creation of cultures of accountability. Studer Group works with hundreds of healthcare organizations worldwide teaching them how to achieve, sustain, and accelerate exceptional clinical, operational, and financial outcomes. We work to bring structure and focus to organizations through the creation of cultures in which people hold themselves accountable and help set them up to be able to execute quickly. By installing an execution framework called Evidence-Based Leadership^{SM}, organizations are able to align goals, actions, and processes. This framework creates the foundation that enables transformation in this era of continuous change. We also help them foster better integration with physicians and other service providers in order to create a smooth continuum of patient-centered care.

STUDER GROUP COACHING:

Healthcare Organization Coaching

As value-based purchasing changes the healthcare landscape forever, organizations need to execute quickly and consistently, achieve better outcomes across the board, and sustain improvements year after year. Studer Group's team of performance experts has hands-on experience in all aspects of achieving breakthrough results. They provide the strategic thinking, the Evidence-Based Leadership framework, the practical tactics, and the ongoing support to help our partners excel in this high-pressure environment. Our performance experts work with a variety of organizations, from academic medical centers to large healthcare systems to small rural hospitals.

Emergency Department Coaching

With public reporting of data, healthcare organizations can no longer accept crowded Emergency Departments and long patient wait times. Our team of ED coach experts will partner with you to implement best practices, proven tools, and tactics using our Evidence-Based Leadership approach to improve results in the Emergency Department that stretch or impact across the entire organization. Key deliverables include improving flow, decreasing staff turnover, increasing employee, physician, and patient satisfaction, decreasing door-to-doctor times, reducing left without being seen rates, increasing up-front cash collections, and increasing patient volumes and revenue.

<u>Physician Integration & Partnership Coaching</u>
Physician integration is critical to an organization's ability to run smoothly and efficiently today and to do more with less in a financially challenging future. Studer Group coaches diagnose how aligned physicians are with your mission and goals, train you on how to effectively provide performance feedback, and help physicians develop the skills they need to prevent burnout. The goal is to help physicians become engaged, enthusiastic partners in the truest sense of the word—which optimizes HCAHPS results and creates a better continuum of high-quality patient care.

To learn more about Studer Group coaching, visit www.studergroup.com.

BOOKS: categorized by audience

Senior Leaders & Physicians
A Culture of High Performance: Achieving Higher Quality at a Lower Cost—A must-have for any leader struggling to shore up margins while sustaining an organization that's a great place for employees to work, physicians to practice medicine, and patients to receive care.

Engaging Physicians: A Manual to Physician Partnership—A tactical and passionate road map for physician collaboration to generate organizational high performance, written by Stephen C. Beeson, MD.

Straight A Leadership: Alignment, Action, Accountability—A guide that will help you identify gaps in alignment, action, and accountability, create a plan to fill them, and become a more resourceful, agile, high-performing organization, written by Quint Studer.

Excellence with an Edge: Practicing Medicine in a Competitive Environment—An insightful book that provides practical tools and techniques you need to know to have a solid grasp of the business side of making a living in healthcare, written by Michael T. Harris, MD.

Physicians
Practicing Excellence: A Physician's Manual to Exceptional Health Care—This book, written by Stephen C. Beeson, MD, is a brilliant guide to implementing physician leadership and behaviors that will create a high-performance workplace.

<u>All Leaders and Healthcare Professionals</u>
The Great Employee Handbook: Making Work and Life Better—
This book is a valuable resource for employees at all levels who want to learn how to handle tough workplace situations—skills that normally come only from a lifetime of experience. *Wall Street Journal* bestselling author Quint Studer has pulled together the best insights gained from working with thousands of employees during his career.

Oh No…Not More of That Fluffy Stuff! The Power of Engagement—A funny, heartfelt, and inspiring look at what it takes to overcome huge obstacles and tap into the passion that fuels our best work. A follow-up to Bluni's wildly popular *Inspired Nurse*, it's filled with aha moments and practical exercises that help readers become happier, more excited, and more connected to the meaning in their daily lives.

Hey Cupcake! We Are ALL Leaders—This book helps the reader to manage change (it involves the acronym BARF) and delivers solid advice on topics from dealing with problem employees (Queens, Poisoners, and Calamity Janes) to owning the tough decisions to telling others what you really need.

Hardwiring Excellence—A *Business Week* bestseller, this book is a road map to creating and sustaining a "Culture of Service and Operational Excellence" that drives bottom-line results. Written by Quint Studer.

Results That Last—A *Wall Street Journal* bestseller by Quint Studer that teaches leaders in every industry how to apply his tactics and strategies to their own organizations to build a corporate culture that consistently reaches and exceeds its goals.

Hardwiring Flow: Systems and Processes for Seamless Patient Care—Drs. Thom Mayer and Kirk Jensen delve into one of the most critical issues facing healthcare leaders today: patient flow.

Eat That Cookie!: Make Workplace Positivity Pay Off...for Individuals, Teams, and Organizations—Written by Liz Jazwiec, RN, this book is funny, inspiring, relatable, and is packed with realistic, down-to-earth tactics to infuse positivity into your culture.

"I'm Sorry to Hear That..." Real-Life Responses to Patients' 101 Most Common Complaints About Health Care—When you respond to a patient's complaint, you are responding to the patient's sense of helplessness and anxiety. The service recovery scripts offered in this book can help you recover a patient's confidence in you and your organization. Authored by Susan Keane Baker and Leslie Bank.

101 Answers to Questions Leaders Ask—By Quint Studer and Studer Group coaches, offers practical, prescriptive solutions to some of the many questions he's received from healthcare leaders around the country.

Over Our Heads: An Analogy on Healthcare, Good Intentions, and Unforeseen Consequences—This book, written by Rulon F. Stacey, PhD, FACHE, uses a grocery store analogy to illustrate how government intervention leads to economic crisis and, eventually, collapse.

Nurse Leaders and Nurses

The Nurse Leader Handbook: The Art and Science of Nurse Leadership—By Studer Group senior nursing and physician leaders from across the country, this book is filled with knowledge that provides nurse leaders with a solid foundation for success. It also serves as a reference they can revisit again and again when they have questions or need a quick refresher course in a particular area of the job.

Inspired Nurse and *Inspired Journal*—By Rich Bluni, RN, helps maintain and recapture the inspiration nurses felt at the start of their journey with action-oriented "spiritual stretches" and stories that illuminate those sacred moments we all experience.

Emergency Department Team

Excellence in the Emergency Department: How to Get Results—A book by Stephanie Baker, RN, CEN, MBA, is filled with proven, easy-to-implement, step-by-step instructions that will help you move your Emergency Department forward.

For more information about books and other resources, visit www.firestarterpublishing.com.

INSIGHTS FROM STUDER GROUP EXPERTS:

Quick, to-the-point articles from founder Quint Studer and other Studer Group experts provide critical information and incisive commentary on hot industry issues.

To read the latest Insights, as well as archived editions, visit www.studergroup.com.

SOFTWARE SOLUTIONS:

Leader Evaluation Manager®: Results through Focus and Accountability
Organizations need a way to align goals for their leaders, create a sense of urgency around the most important ones, and hold leaders accountable for meeting their targets. Value-based purchasing, which forces you to improve faster and faster, makes this more critical than ever. Studer Group's Leader Evaluation Manager automates the goal setting and performance review process for all leaders.

To learn more, please visit www.studergroup.com.

INSTITUTES:

Taking You and Your Organization to the Next Level

At this two-day institute, leaders learn tactics proven to help them quickly move results in the most critical areas: HCAHPS, Core Measures, preventable readmissions, hospital-acquired conditions, and more. They walk away with a clear action plan that yields measurable improvement within 90 days. Even more important, they learn how to implement these tactics in the context of our Evidence-Based Leadership framework so they can execute quickly and consistently and sustain the results over time.

Excellence in the Emergency Department: Hardwiring Flow & Patient Experience

Crowded Emergency Departments and long patient wait times are no longer acceptable, especially with public reporting of data in the near future. We can predict with great accuracy when lulls and peak times will be, and we know exactly how to improve flow and provide better quality care. This institute will reveal a few simple, hard-hitting tactics that solve the most pressing ED problems *and* create better clinical quality and patient perception of care throughout the entire hospital stay.

The Physician Partnership Institute: A Path to Alignment, Engagement, and Integration

The changes mandated by health reform make it clear: There will surely be some sort of "marriage" between hospitals and physicians. Regardless of what form it takes, we must start laying the groundwork for a rewarding partnership now. Learn our comprehensive methodology for getting physicians aligned with, engaged in, and committed to your organization so that everyone is working together to provide the best possible clinical care, improve HCAHPS and CGCAHPS results, increase patient loyalty, and gain market share.

<u>What's Right in Health Care</u>®
One of the largest healthcare peer-to-peer learning conferences in the nation, What's Right in Health Care brings organizations together to share ideas that have been proven to make healthcare better. Thousands of leaders attend this institute every year to network with their peers, to hear top industry experts speak, and to learn tactical best practices that allow them to accelerate and sustain performance.

To review a listing of Studer Group institutes or to register for an institute, visit www.studergroup.com/institutes.

For information on Continuing Education Credits, visit www.studergroup.com/cmecredits.

Acknowledgments

I would like to offer my (for once) humble gratitude to the following:

Quint Studer, the person who not only understood the importance of engaging people's hearts as well as their minds, but who also engaged my heart in connecting to healthcare's birthright of making people feel better. Our longstanding friendship has served as a great support for all I do. I will always be grateful for the blessing that is Quint Studer.

Don Dean, this gentle genius from whom I have learned so much. His commitment to improving service excellence is unmatched by anyone. Patients in hospitals everywhere have better experiences because somewhere, somehow, someone who works there has undoubtedly been influenced by Don's work. I am glad that to this day he remains a close friend of mine.

Bill Hejna, who does not get enough credit for his contributions to service excellence. Nevertheless, some of the best ideas ever implemented stemmed from his insight and vision. He understands all aspects of healthcare: leadership, team, patient, and family. His sensitivity and compassion make him not only a great humanitarian, but also the dearest of friends. He is also the reason why there are three books in this series—it was Bill's advice as I was writing *Cookie* to consider making the series a trilogy!

Mark Albarian, who remains my closest confidant and biggest supporter. As is true with most lifelong friends, although we don't see each other as often as we would like or chat as much as we want to, just knowing that he is only a phone call away brings much happiness and comfort in my life. When we do spend time together, I am immediately reminded of how blessed I am to have him as a friend. Without question, he is the reason I started this chapter of my career and for that I will be forever grateful.

Bekki Kennedy for her encouragement of this crazy trilogy of cookies, cupcakes, and now pie. I am so appreciative of her support in making sure that the books stayed true to me. I am very thankful that she allowed my voice to come through on each and every page. It has been a true pleasure getting to collaborate with her over these past several years.

Jamie Stewart from Fire Starter Publishing, who I believe was more enthusiastic about this third book than I was! Her promotion and assistance have been so valuable, and it was wonderful working together.

Dottie DeHart and her team—Anna Campbell, Ashley Lamb, Lindsay Miller, and Meghan Waters—for enduring another round of editing with me. I am so grateful for your patience with me. Your extraordinary work makes my work seem easy.

Rich Bluni, who not only "inspires" people across the country, but also motivates me to want to do better. I am so privileged and blessed to have him in my life. He is an amazing supporter, my closest colleague, and most importantly, a cherished friend.

Kathleen Collins, my fearless administrative assistant whose loyalty has no bounds. Without her support both professionally and personally, I would not be able to do the work that I love. Thank you from the bottom of my heart for being in my corner every single day.

And as always, my amazing friends and family whose encouragement and support are as steadfast and as dependable as the sun rising in the morning. I am so fortunate to have a sister who not only gets excited when I am working on a new book, but who also contributes stories for them. Thank you, Donna! I am also blessed with nieces and a nephew who bring joy into my life and make me proud every day. I want to do the same for you, Cathy, Lauren, and Tyler.

Finally, to my parents, Bob and Marcy Ross, who have provided me with the love, support, and education to be able to do work that I love. I know for a fact that my parents sacrificed so that my sister and I could have exceptional educations. It is that foundation that has led to so many opportunities for us. I am very lucky to have had such outstanding, loving, wonderful parents; I will *never* be able to thank them enough.

About the Author

An internationally renowned speaker, strategist, and author, Liz Jazwiec consistently ranks amongst the best of the best. She is the award-winning author of the best-selling books *Eat That Cookie!: Make Workplace Positivity Pay Off...for Individuals, Teams and Organizations* and *Hey Cupcake! We Are ALL Leaders.* As the president and founder of Liz, inc., she has shared her passion for leadership, engagement, and service with fans and followers from many different backgrounds and industries.

Liz has also been a vice president of patient care, Emergency Department director, executive search professional, and organizational development leader. Her work at Holy Cross Hospital in Chicago, Illinois, contributed to the organization's being recognized for its award-winning patient satisfaction. Today Liz uses all of her experience and expertise to inspire organizations committed to building a culture where service excellence is driven by strong leaders and engaged employees.

Audiences describe Liz's presentations as uplifting, motivational, and fun. They also respect her practical and experience-based style. You're sure to enjoy her creative and viable suggestions for addressing some of the difficult issues facing today's leaders and their organizations. You may contact Liz at www.LizJazz.com.

How to Order Additional Copies of

Service Excellence Is as Easy as PIE
(Perception Is Everything)

Hey Cupcake!
We Are ALL Leaders

Eat That Cookie!
Make Workplace Positivity Pay Off...For
Individuals, Teams and Organizations

Orders may be placed:

Online at:
www.firestarterpublishing.com
www.studergroup.com

By phone at: 866-354-3473

By mail at: Fire Starter Publishing
913 Gulf Breeze Parkway, Suite 6
Gulf Breeze, FL 32561

(Bulk discounts are available.)